Since 1944

Patsy's 1954

Patsy's®

Since 1944

ITALIAN FAMILY COOKBOOK

SAL J. SCOGNAMILLO

PHOTOGRAPHS BY JEFFREY GURWIN

ST. MARTIN'S PRESS ❧ NEW YORK

PATSY'S ITALIAN FAMILY COOKBOOK. Copyright © 2015 by Sal J. Scognamillo. Foreword © 2015 by Ben Stiller. All rights reserved. Printed in China. For information, address St. Martin's Press, 175 Fifth Avenue, New York, N.Y. 10010.

www.stmartins.com

Food photography by Jeffrey Gurwin. All other photographs courtesy of Sal Scognamillo.

Designed by James Sinclair
Production Manager: Adriana Coada

The Library of Congress Cataloging-in-Publication Data is available upon request.

ISBN 978-1-250-03939-2 (hardcover)
ISBN 978-1-250-03940-8 (e-book)

St. Martin's Press books may be purchased for educational, business, or promotional use. For information on bulk purchases, please contact the Macmillan Corporate and Premium Sales Department at 1-800-221-7945, extension 5442, or write to specialmarkets@macmillan.com.

First Edition: March 2015

10 9 8 7 6 5 4 3 2 1

This book is dedicated to my beloved Aunt Anna—sweet, caring, and always generous. Love was the main ingredient in every dish she served.

And to my father, Joe Scognamillo—my inspiration and my hero.

Contents

Foreword

by Ben Stiller

"What can I make for you tonight?"

Joe Scognamillo at Patsy's in the early 1980s.

When I think of growing up in New York, one of the brightest, happiest memories that comes to mind is of a warm, loving Scognamillo asking me what I wanted to eat. "Would you like pasta? Veal Parmigiana?" I was in heaven.

As a kid, I spent a lot of time at Patsy's. In fact, we were there for so many dinner and family celebrations that I don't actually remember the first time I stepped through the doors of the famed restaurant on West Fifty-sixth Street.

My mom and dad, Anne Meara and Jerry Stiller, introduced my sister Amy and me to Patsy's, the place where they held court, like scores of other entertainers, after an appearance in a nearby theater, studio, or nightclub. It became a ritual for them after performing live in front of 40 million people on *The Ed Sullivan Show,* whose theater was right around the corner. The waiters were impeccably dressed, moving like locomotives through the dining room, and everyone paid incredible attention to detail. Titans of industry, entertainers, people on a special first-time trip to New York, all came through, and all, it seemed, felt the same way—*special*. Despite its formality, the overwhelming feeling I got whenever we visited Patsy's was one of *warmth*. Even as an eight-year-old, I could see that the warmth and gratitude exuded by Patsy, his wife, and their children (Anna and Joe) weren't reserved exclusively for us. *Everyone* who came to Patsy's for dinner was treated like family.

In a world where the importance of history and tradition seems to have diminished, I'm delighted that the Patsy's of my youth endures. For years, my parents and the Scognamillos have enjoyed a genuine affection for each other, and many important memories from my childhood are rooted in the time we shared at Patsy's. That personal bond is important to me especially now as I am able to take my kids there for special occasions. I guess it is not surprising my kids love the food there as much as we did. And it's comforting to know that Joe, Rose, Sal, Frank, and the staff—many of whom were very young waiters when I was a child—are still there. This remarkable continuity, and our lifelong friendship with the Scognamillo family has created a wonderful bridge of connection that all our families share.

And so, the tradition continues . . . and with it, a delightful new cookbook illustrating more recipes from Patsy's extensive menu. And the collection includes dishes from the family's personal recipe file. I hope you'll cherish and enjoy this book as much as I do!

Even as other things in New York City change from day to day, I can rest easy knowing there's a good chance that one thing will always stay the same: the exceptional "family-first" philosophy at Patsy's Italian Restaurant. I look forward to many more years of friendship. I am sure that one day in the future I'll arrive at Patsy's to have Sal greet me at the front counter, and see his son Peter emerge from the kitchen wearing a chef's cap to ask the question I've heard so many times, *"What can I make for you tonight?"*

Joe Scognamillo
and Ben Stiller

Introduction

⟨⟨⟩⟩

Patsy's has stood on West Fifty-sixth Street near Broadway for over seventy years and counting, owned by the same family for the entire period, which must be some kind of a record in the "here today, gone tomorrow" Manhattan restaurant world. Four generations of Scognamillos have worked here: My grandfather, Pasquale (everyone called him Patsy); my dad, Joe; me; my cousin, Frank; his son, Paul; and my sons, Joseph and Peter. (Actually, Peter is still too young to be working, but he spends an awful lot of time hanging out in the kitchen.) You'll find Joe in the front of the house, and my mother Rose answering the phone. Patsy's is about the food, but also family. Of the parade of celebrities who have dined at Patsy's, many have literally become family. And of these, no one was more an honorary Scognamillo than Frank Sinatra, who my grandfather met in the early forties at the beginning of "Old Blue Eye's" singing career.

When people ask me the secret to our business's longevity, I say that, along with the food, it's because we've stayed small—and that people know they will be treated like welcome friends. Don't be confused by other eating establishments in New York with similar names. Our Patsy's Italian restaurant is and always has been, owned by the Scognamillo family.

Patsy's Italian Family Cookbook expresses that sense of tradition. I share two kinds of recipes, the ones that have made us one of the best "red sauce" restaurants in New York City and our favorite fam-

Postcards of the restaurant, used from the 1950s through the early 1980s.

ily dishes that we serve at home. You'll find special fare that we make for holiday feasts as well as the simple food that we make on our nights off. Some of these were transcribed from handwritten index cards that have been handed down from a dear relative. These recipes make me smile—when I taste my Aunt Anna's Chicken Gravy, I can see her at the stove.

My dad Joe's first Communion, with his godfather, Uncle Vincent, about 1940.

Italian Americans, took the "feast" part literally. Because the restaurant was open on Sundays but closed on Mondays, we had our celebration dinner on Easter Monday. (We are now open seven days a week, but closed on a few holidays.) We'd gather at my grandparents' home in Forest Hills, Queens. To show you the importance of food in our family, every floor of this house had a kitchen. (Even at Patsy's Restaurant we have an upstairs and a downstairs kitchen, which may be because my grandfather was used to cooking that way!) The dinners were served in the basement because we had so many people we wouldn't fit in the dining room. If we couldn't all fit at the tables, as often happened, we would eat in shifts. Before the meal, my grandfather would take a palm saved from Palm Sunday's service, dip it in holy water, and bless everyone at the table with a shake of the water.

While my memories of holiday parties are vivid, so are my recollections of everyday meals. Then, as now, we didn't have a lot of time to spend over the stove, so we had a lot of delicious meals that were quickly prepared. Because my grandparents were so poor, both in Naples and for the first part of their

From the days when my grandfather owned his first restaurant, the Sorrento, on West Forty-ninth Street, we served foods with Old World flavors. At that time Italians were pigeonholed into certain professions and musicians, florists, and tailors came for the Southern Italian food they couldn't get anywhere else. Patsy and his wife Concetta would make the wonderful food of Naples, and customers meant it when they said it tasted "just like Mamma's." When Easter and Christmas came, specialties of the season (such as pastiera Napolitana and baccalà salad, both recipes that you'll find in this book) were on the menu.

In the Catholic faith, the most enjoyable holidays are called feast days, and my family, like most

My dad and me in the kitchen, 1985—when I started my training.

American life, we were taught to never, ever waste food. My grandmother Concetta showed us all how to turn leftover bread into bread crumbs, add hot milk to last night's coffee for breakfast, or cook leftover pasta with eggs to make a frittata for dinner. Some of my favorite dishes have very humble ingredients like cauliflower and Brussels sprouts, stretched with some ingenuity to make a meal.

Every day at Patsy's, I sit down with my relatives and extended family and share a meal about 3 p.m., between lunch and dinner services. This is the same kind of meal that I would have if I were at home, spending quality time and catching up. We'll order off the menu, or maybe one of us will make a home-style dish like roast chicken, or a family recipe.

Yes, running a restaurant is hard work, but there's a lot of love and laughter. If you don't think it's fun seeing Billy Joel stand and sing "Happy Birthday" to a surprised guest, think again. Or staying open so Michael Bublé can have a party after a concert in Sinatra's old hangout, the upstairs dining room. Or watching Frankie Valli tear into a bowl of spaghetti and meatballs. Or still, every day, have people ask where Sinatra sat or about his favorite dishes—arugula salad without garlic and very crisp, very thinly pounded veal Milanese.

There is a unique energy at Patsy's that only comes with years in the business, serving up good food and good times. A customer said to me once, "Eating at Patsy's reminds me of seeing Tony Bennett in concert. You realize the guy's been fantastic for years, but it's the skill that comes from doing it day in and day out that makes him so great." That's the way it is with Patsy's.

But there is another kind of energy at the restaurant, the one generated when good friends and family get together for a great meal. Walking around the tables to chat with our customers, I have made more than a few invaluable friendships. Many years ago, my good buddy Tony Danza started calling me "My Pal Sal." This three-word nickname has stuck and I hope it isn't too long before you and your family come in and become part of our family.

—*Sal J. Scognamillo*

The Patsy's crew, 1991.

APPETIZERS

Home Made Antipasto	1.30
Assorted Italian Antipasto	1.00
Shrimps Cocktail	.80
Prosciutto (Italian Ham)	1.00
Tuna Fish in Olive Oil	.90
Italian Salami	.90
Pimento and Anchovies	.90
Celery and Olives	.80
Prosciutto & Melon (In Season)	1.25

SOUPS

Consomme Romana	.70	Spinach in Brodo	.75
Plain Consomme	.40	Noodles Soup	.75
Pavese Soup	.80	Escarole Soup	.75

SPAGHETTI & RAVIOLI

Ziti a la Patsy	1.25	Spaghetti Provenzale	1.25
Spaghetti Tomato Sauce	1.20	Spaghetti Meat Balls	1.35
Spaghetti Meat Sauce	1.25	Linguini Clam Sauce	1.35
Spaghetti Marinara	1.20	Linguini Marechaire	1.40
Spaghetti Clam Sauce	1.30	Home Made Lasagnette	1.20
Spaghetti Garlic & Oil	1.15	Home Made Ravioli	1.20
Spaghetti Mushroom Sauce			1.25

Extra Sauce 25¢

EGGS AND OMELETTES

Plain Omelette	1.00	Eggs al Purgatorio	1.30
Omelette with Salami	1.30	Mushrooms Omelette	1.30
Omelette with Italian Ham			1.30
Omelette with Mozzarella			1.30
Scrambled Eggs with Sausages			1.75

SEA FOOD

Lobster Fra Diavolo		Mussels a la Marinara	1.40
Shrimps Marinara	1.75	Whiting in Cassuola	1.75
Clams a la Posillipo	1.75	Cassuola Di Pesce	2.50
Squids in Cassuola	1.55	Black Sea Bass (Broiled)	1.95
Mixed Fr. Fish all'Italiana			2.25

FRESH VEGETABLES IN SEASON

Bitter Broccoli Affogati	1.50	Eggplant Parmisan	1.30
String Beans Marinara	1.30	Escarole Saute	1.20
Broccoli Saute	1.25	Spinach Saute	1.20
Fresh Asparagus with Butter			1.00
Fresh Asparagus Parmigiana			1.00

POTATOES

Italian Stewed	.70	French Fried	.70
Potatoes Croquette			.90

ENTREES

Whole Chicken Cacciatora			5.00
Half Chicken Cacciatora			2.75
Beef Scallops with Mushrooms			4.50
Veal Scallopine a la Patsy			2.00
Veal Scallopine with Mushrooms			1.95
Veal Scallopine with Peppers			1.80
Veal Scallopine with Peppers and Mushrooms			2.25
Veal Kidney Saute with Mushrooms			1.90
Veal Scallopine Francese	2.00	Veal Chop Pizzaiola	1.75
Veal Cutlet Milanaise	1.50	Calf's Liver Saute	2.00
Veal Cutlet Parmigiana	1.85	Calf's Liver Veneziana	2.65
Chicken Liver Cacciatora	2.75	Calf's Brains Saute	1.75
Pork Chop Pizzaiola	1.75	Calf's Brains Arreganata	1.75
Sausage Pizzaiola with Peppers			1.90
Spedino alla Romana			1.60
Mozzarella in Carrozza			1.60
Sirloin Steak Pizzaiola			5.50
Sirloin Steak Pizzaiola, Mushrooms & Peppers			6.00

FROM THE GRILL

Sirloin Steak	4.75	Broiled Lamb Chops (2)	3.10
Whole Broiled Chicken	4.50	Broiled Veal Chop	1.50
Half Broiled Chicken	2.25	Broiled Pork Chop	1.50
Broiled Calf's Liver			2.00

Above Orders with Vegetable 15¢ Extra

SALADS

Mixed Green Salad	.85	Romaine Salad	.70
Combination Salad	.95	Lettuce and Tomatoes	.75
Sliced Tomatoes			.70

CHEESE

Imported Provolone	.95	Bel Paese	.95
Gorgonzola	.95	Mozzarella	.95
Ricotta			.95

DESSERTS

Pastry	.35	Spumoni Ice Cream	.35
Cheese Cake	.45	Large Bisquit Tortoni	.35
Fresh Fruit in Season			

BEVERAGES

Coffee	.15	Tea	.15
Demitasse	.15	Iced Coffee or Tea	.35

A Patsy's souvenir menu from the early 1950s.

Italian Cuisine à la Patsy's

Patsy's proudly calls itself a "red sauce" restaurant. This kind of Italian American restaurant features many dishes topped in tomato sauce, but of course, the quality of the place clearly relies on the excellence of the sauce. All of our recipes are rooted in traditional Italian cooking, which is based on seasonal produce (by necessity, because there was no refrigeration) and local products (a cheese made in the next town was considered foreign). You'll find items on the menu that we have been making since the very first day my grandfather opened Patsy's in 1944.

This means that we have been cooking our food the same way for decades. Occasionally we will put a more contemporary item on the menu (we love balsamic vinegar as much as the rest of the world), but for the most part, our customers come to Patsy's for a taste of Old Italy. And we're happy to provide that. My grandfather had a saying, "You aren't born round and die square," which meant that you don't change much from the cradle to the grave. I think he also meant to apply that to Patsy's. Another way of thinking is, as we say in New York, "If it ain't broken, don't fix it." So many of the recipes we serve at the restaurant are based on ones that my family brought from Naples, and are just bigger batches of what Grandma Concetta, Aunt Anna, and others cooked for their families at home.

My father Joe learned how to cook from his father Patsy, and they passed on what they know to me. I am doing the same with my sons. Here are tips and advice on the cooking techniques and ingredients that we use every day so your home-cooked meals will taste like a Scognamillo cooked it.

Big Family, Big Pans

I am used to cooking for lots of people at the restaurant, and I think in large quantities. But we have a big family, too, and a holiday meal is usually cooked for at least two dozen people. When you are making a dinner party (or even a weeknight meal) for more

The party for my grandparents' twenty-fifth wedding anniversary.

than a couple of people, a too-small skillet can defeat your efforts.

Simply put, you need utensils large enough for the job. With a medium, 9-inch-diameter skillet, many recipes would have to be cooked in batches. Every kitchen should have a 12- to 14-inch-diameter, heavy-gauge skillet that can hold four servings (fish fillets, chicken breast halves, chops, or what have you) at once. When food is crowded in a small skillet, it creates steam that inhibits browning, and browned food tastes best.

Two other cooking vessels will help cook the recipes in this book. A 6- to 7-quart Dutch oven, preferably enameled cast iron, is another must for braises and stews. (I like an oval one because it holds a chicken more efficiently than the round pot.) Another item that comes in handy is a flameproof 9 by 13-inch baking dish that can go under a broiler. Again, an enameled cast-iron dish will work beautifully. Some of my favorite recipes are finished with a blast of direct heat at the end of cooking to give the food a irresistible crusty surface.

A lot of our customers have small Manhattan kitchens with limited storage space. But even if you have to store these utensils underneath your bed, it is worth the slight inconvenience.

Bread Crumbs

We use plain dried bread crumbs, sold in a box at the market, for many dishes. They are handy and do the trick. To be in control of the recipe's seasoning, don't use the ones that are seasoned with herbs or cheese.

Many of our recipes use the homemade Seasoned Bread Crumbs on page 14. These have more texture and flavor than the store-bought version and can be stored in the freezer so you have them ready when you need them.

Olive Oil

One of the essentials in Italian cooking, choose your olive oil carefully. We use two olive oil varieties at Patsy's and at home, too.

Extra-virgin olive oil is mechanically pressed from green olives without heat, and the contact with the skins gives the oil its color. (Truthfully, the "extra" in the name doesn't mean much, only that the oil is very pure.) This first pressing is done without heat, so you will see "cold-pressed" on some labels. The very best and most expensive olive oil is estate-bottled, like wine, which means that the olives are grown, processed, and usually bottled from the same location. We use a top-quality olive oil that has a moderately heavy body and distinct, but not overpowering, olive flavor. This oil is reserved for recipes where the olive flavor should be noticeable, as in a pasta sauce or salad dressing. When choosing olive oil for your own use, taste it before using whenever possible. There are so many characteristics that define olive oil—peppery or grassy flavors, viscosity, and color—that it really boils down to personal taste.

The flavor of olive oil weakens when heated. For that reason, we also use a regular (formerly called pure) olive oil for cooking, or when we want the olive taste to be more neutral. Processed from the residual first pressing olives, this is the clear yellow olive oil that you see at the market (and for years, the only kind you could buy in America).

Because heat and sunlight adversely affects the keeping qualities of olive oil, store it in a cool, dark place, but not the refrigerator, where it will solidify.

Olive oil doesn't last much more than a year, and is really best within a couple of months of bottling. Some producers pack their olive oil in dark glass bottles to block the sunlight, but everyone we know uses olive oil so rapidly that it doesn't really get a chance to go rancid. But keeping it near a hot stove isn't a good idea.

Garlic

The Jekyll and Hyde of Italian cooking, garlic can be very friendly or mean and nasty. Like a person, garlic treated with respect will behave. We are very sensitive about garlic because our dear friend Frank Sinatra didn't like it, so we had to be sure that the flavor was subtle (if used at all) in the food we cooked for him. (Maybe it was because he didn't want his breath to offend someone that he was singing duets with?)

The main problem with garlic is that it burns easily, especially when it is minced, which is the most common way of prepping it. Scorched garlic is dark brown, with a bitter, strong flavor. Too many cooks, even good ones, heat the oil in the cooking utensil, and then add the garlic, which immediately starts to overcook when it hits the hot oil. To help curb that problem, cook the garlic more slowly: Put the oil and garlic in the utensil at the beginning of cooking, and heat them together over medium until the garlic is golden and gives off its aroma, in about 2 minutes. At this point, you can add the other ingredients. Problem solved.

A trick I learned from Grandma Concetta is to use garlic halves instead of minced garlic for a mellower, gentler flavor. Once the garlic halves have infused the food (usually a sauce), retrieve and discard them. We do this in some recipes.

Herbs

When Patsy opened the restaurant in the 1940s, the only fresh herb that you could get with any regularity was parsley. Even then, he didn't like food that was heavily dosed with dried oregano, a flavor that has unfortunately became associated with Italian cooking. That may be true, but it isn't the Italian cooking that I know. I use a very light hand with dried oregano.

I love fresh basil. It has an irresistible spicy aroma and delicate texture that goes beautifully with many of our recipes, especially those with tomato sauce. Basil used to be a summer crop, but now it is available year-round. If your supermarket doesn't have it, check your local Asian market, or look for boxes of basil at Trader Joe's. The basil leaves are very tender, and will turn black in the refrigerator if unprotected. Cut off the ends of the basil stems and stand the bunch in a short glass of water. Cover the leaves with a plastic bag and store in the fridge. Protected in this way, the basil will stay fresh for a few days. If you instinctively pop the bunch into the refrigerator vegetable drawer, it will wilt overnight.

My grandmother never chopped basil, believing that chopping left the herb's precious aroma behind on the board. Instead, she would tear it into small pieces before dropping it into the cooking food. I respect her views, but chopping is a lot quicker. However, use a sharp knife because if the leaves are bruised instead of cleanly cut, they will discolor.

Before chopping, the basil must be cleaned and completely dried. Pick the leaves from the stems, rinse well to remove any sand, and dry in a salad spinner or pat them dry on paper towels.

For most recipes, coarsely chopped basil works fine. However, when I want to use basil as a garnish, I'll cut it into thin shreds called a *chiffonade*. These delicate shreds fall evenly and lightly over the food, and look better than regular chopped basil. **To make basil chiffonade,** stack a few leaves and roll them into a thick cylinder. Cut the cylinder crosswise into very thin shreds, less than ¹⁄₁₆ inch wide. As with chopped basil, be sure your knife is good and sharp to avoid discolored shreds. Now the chiffonade can be scattered over each serving for a very nice visual effect.

Prepared Pork Products

Back in Naples, meat was preserved to use throughout the year until the next slaughter. Pork was easy to raise and maintain, so you will find a lot of processed pork in the old recipes. Just a little of these frankly fatty products add a lot of flavor to a dish.

Sopressata is a firm, narrow, version of salami, and is seasoned either sweet or hot.

Pancetta is the Italian version of bacon, but the pork belly is not smoked, and it is rolled into a cylinder. Be sure to remove the casings from sopressata and pancetta before using.

Prosciutto is an air-cured ham, and while it is a specialty of Parma, there are good domestic versions, too.

The important thing about cooking with pancetta and prosciutto is that it should not be sliced too thin. These meats should retain some texture in the food. Overzealous deli workers are used to carving them into paper-thin sheets. Ask them to cut the meat into slices ⅛ to ¼ inch thick, and then dice them as needed at home. Some markets also carry precut prosciutto and pancetta specifically for cooking.

Seasoning

We use plain table salt at Patsy's. In my opinion, salt is salt, and I don't fuss with sea or kosher salt. The peppercorns are black and freshly ground.

I usually don't season the meat in a dish because I like it to pick up the seasoning from the sauce. Grilled and roasted meats are an exception. Also, your guests can season the food to taste at the table.

Italian Cheeses

We cook with a trio of cheeses that we cannot do without: Parmigiano-Reggiano, mozzarella, and ricotta.

Parmigiano-Reggiano is simply Parmesan cheese, but the very best, imported kind from the region around Parma, Italy. Other countries make Parmesan-style cheese, which is a pale imitation of the real thing, which has an almost nutty flavor, straw-yellow color, and a firm, but not waxy, texture. Authentic Parmesan has "Parmigiano-Reggiano" stamped all over the rind. It should always be freshly grated so it doesn't dry out and lose flavor. Wrapped in foil or plastic wrap, Parmigiano can be stored for a few weeks in the refrigerator. My grandparents sometimes used another hard Italian grating cheese, Grana Padano, and it is a good substitute for Parmigiano-Reggiano if you want to economize. And a few dishes use Pecorino Romano, a sheep's milk cheese, which is sharper than Parmigiano-Reggiano.

Mozzarella is renowned for its melting qualities and creamy texture. Fresh mozzarella simply tastes better than the factory-made processed version, and we only use the fresh kind at Patsy's. This cheese used to be a rarity, but now you can find it at supermarkets. If you can get freshly made mozzarella at a local Italian delicatessen, so much the better. Fresh mozzarella is much softer than processed mozzarella, and it is easier to chop it than shred it. It will only keep in the refrigerator for a couple of days. If you can only get the firmer, processed mozzarella, use it.

Ricotta means "recooked," as this cheese is traditionally made from heated leftover whey. We use fresh ricotta, which has a very delicate texture and flavor different from the processed variety easily available at the supermarket. Fresh ricotta is sold at Italian delicatessens and cheese stores, but I admit that it isn't easy to find. (We drive 50 miles to get ours in New Jersey because our favorite producer doesn't deliver to New York.) You can use supermarket ricotta in these recipes.

Pasta

I wonder how many hundreds of thousands of pasta orders we have served over the years? Here's what I have learned about the mainstay of Italian (and American) cooking.

There are a lot of good pasta companies out there. You can't really say that fresh is better than dried, or vice versa. I will say that I have come to prefer delicate fresh pasta when I am making special pasta dishes for holiday dishes like lasagna or manicotti, or when serving light vegetarian sauces. I have provided a recipe for fresh pasta in case you want to make your own for the "stuffed pastas." But most communities now have a place where you can buy fresh pasta—a natural foods store, Italian delicatessen, or a dedicated pasta shop.

For each pound of pasta, bring at least 3 quarts of salted water to boil in a saucepan over high heat.

How much salt? Enough so that the water actually tastes salty, but not as much as ocean water. Stir in the pasta, being sure that the strands or pieces aren't sticking together. Never add oil to the water because it will slick the pasta during draining and keep the sauce from sticking properly. Cook the pasta according to the package directions until it is al dente. Be sure not to go past this "firm to the bite" stage because, in my recipes, the pasta has one more stage of cooking to go through before serving.

In some cases, a portion of the cooking water, which has picked up some of the starches from the pasta, is scooped out and saved for mixing with the sauce later. Just dip a ladle or heatproof measuring cup into the water before draining the pasta. When the pasta is mixed with thick pesto-like sauces, the reserved liquid is stirred in to loosen and smooth out the sauce.

Another restaurant trick to use at home is to cook the pasta with the sauce to marry the flavors. Return the drained pasta to its cooking pot and add the sauce. Heat over low-to-medium heat, stirring often, and adding the reserved cooking water if asked to do so, until the pasta has absorbed some of the sauce, usually only a minute or two. Now you are ready to serve it up.

Antipasti

—◆—

Meatball-tini

Seasoned Bread Crumbs

Mussels with White Wine and Lemon

Baked Clams

Mussels Marinara

Shrimp Casino

Eggplant Caponata

Eggplant Bruschetta

Eggplant Rollatini

Bruschetta with Baked Figs and Gorgonzola

Meatball-tini

Our customers love appetizers almost as much as they love martinis, so I combined the two favorites to create the Meatball-tini. These mini meatballs (they are no bigger than a thimble) go down easy, and I can eat them like candy. They are used in both the Neapolitan Meatball and Rice Pie (page 171) and Meatball Lasagna (page 175).

MEATBALL-TINI

¾ cup fresh bread crumbs

½ cup whole milk

2 tablespoons extra-virgin olive oil

1 medium yellow onion, finely chopped

6 garlic cloves, finely chopped

3 pounds ground veal

1½ cups freshly grated Parmigiano-Reggiano cheese (about 6 ounces)

3 large eggs

3 large egg yolks, beaten

3 tablespoons finely chopped fresh flat-leaf parsley, plus more for garnish

1 tablespoon finely chopped fresh oregano, or 1 teaspoon dried

2½ teaspoons salt

1 teaspoon freshly ground black pepper

1. To make the mini meatballs: Put the bread crumbs in a small bowl, drizzle with the milk, and let soak and soften for a few minutes.

2. Heat the oil in a large deep skillet over medium-high heat. Add the onion and garlic and cook until they are lightly browned, 3 to 4 minutes. Transfer to a plate and let cool.

3. Using your hands, mix the veal, soaked bread crumbs, and the onion mixture in a large bowl. Add the grated cheese, whole eggs, egg yolks, parsley, oregano, salt, and pepper and mix again until combined.

4. Dust the work surface with about ½ cup of the seasoned bread crumbs. On the bread crumbs, shape about ¾ cup of the meatball mixture into a 1-inch-wide strip. Sprinkle the top of the strip with more seasoned bread crumbs. Cut the strip into ½- to ¾-inch lengths. Transfer the pieces to a large sieve or strainer and sprinkle lightly with bread crumbs to prevent sticking. Rotate the sieve in a circulation motion to toss the strips of meat and form marble-size meatballs. Transfer the meatballs to a baking sheet. Repeat with the remaining meat mixture and bread crumbs.

5. Preheat the oven to 200°F. Line a baking sheet with paper towels and place near the stove.

6. Pour enough oil into a large deep skillet to come 1 inch up the sides. Heat the oil over high heat to 360°F. Working in batches without crowding, and adding more oil as needed, deep-fry the meatballs until browned and cooked through, about 1½ minutes. Using a slotted spoon, transfer to the paper towel–lined baking sheet. Keep the cooked meatballs warm in

2 cups Seasoned Bread Crumbs or Italian-flavored store-bought dried bread crumbs, for dusting

Olive oil, for deep-frying

3 cups Vodka Sauce (see page 122), heated

Pimiento-stuffed green olives, speared onto toothpicks, for garnish

the oven while frying the rest. (The meatballs can be cooled, packed into 1-gallon plastic storage bags, and refrigerated for up to 2 days or frozen for up to 2 months. Reheat in a 350°F oven for about 10 minutes before using.)

7. For each serving, place a portion of the meatballs in a martini glass. Garnish with parsley and green olives on spears. Serve ramekins of the vodka sauce on the side for dipping the meatballs.

◆ Seasoned Bread Crumbs ◆

MAKES ABOUT 2 CUPS

This is one of the "secret ingredients" in Patsy's kitchens, and a recipe that every Italian grandmother knows by heart. It takes day-old bread and mixes it with a few ingredients to become something special, an all-purpose ingredient that can be used as a coating, binder, and even toasted as a pasta topping. The crumbs keep for a few days in the refrigerator.

8 ounces stale Italian bread (about 1/2 small loaf), cut into large chunks

1/4 cup finely chopped fresh flat-leaf parsley

2 tablespoons freshly grated Parmigiano-Reggiano cheese

1 garlic clove, minced

1/2 teaspoon dried oregano

3 tablespoons olive oil

Salt and freshly ground black pepper

Process the bread chunks in a food processor until they form fine crumbs. (Or process the bread in a blender in batches.) Transfer to a large bowl. Add the parsley, grated cheese, garlic, and oregano and mix well. Gradually stir in the oil to thoroughly moisten the crumbs. Season to taste with salt and pepper. (The crumbs can be refrigerated in a 1-gallon zip-top plastic bag for up to 5 days.)

Mussels with White Wine and Lemon

A bowl of plump mussels in a fragrant sauce is a great way to start a meal. This sauce is especially good, and you won't want to waste a drop, so be sure to serve the mussels with toasted bread for sopping.

2 pounds cultivated mussels, such as Prince Edward Island (see Note)

2 cups cold water

¼ cup extra-virgin olive oil

8 garlic cloves, peeled and thinly sliced

¼ cup dry white wine

⅓ cup plus 1 tablespoon fresh lemon juice

2 scallions (white and green parts), thinly sliced

1 tablespoon finely chopped fresh flat-leaf parsley

½ teaspoon dried oregano

Freshly ground black pepper

Sliced Italian bread, toasted in a broiler or on a grill, for serving

1. Put the mussels in a large pot and add the water. Cover and bring to a boil over high heat. Cook just until the shells open, about 5 minutes. Using a slotted spoon, transfer the opened mussels to a colander, discarding any unopened mussels. Reserve the cooking liquid.

2. Line a wire strainer with moistened paper towels and set over medium bowl. Strain the cooking liquid through the strainer. Measure and reserve 2 cups of the strained liquid. (You can cool, cover, and freeze the remaining mussel cooking liquid for another use or as a fish stock.) Wash and dry the pot.

3. Heat the oil and garlic together in pot over medium heat, stirring often, until the garlic is golden. Add the reserved cooking liquid along with the wine, lemon juice, scallions, parsley, and oregano. Bring to a boil over high heat and cook until the sauce has thickened lightly, about 3 minutes. Season to taste with pepper. Add the mussels, cover, and cook until reheated, about 3 minutes more.

4. Using tongs, divide the mussels evenly among four soup bowls, and ladle in the sauce. Serve hot, with the toasted bread.

NOTE: Cultivated mussels just need to be rinsed before cooking. For wild mussels, using pliers, pull off and discard the hairy "beards" sticking out of the shells, then scrub and soak them in a big pot of salted ice water for an hour or two, then drain. After cooking, when straining the liquid, leave any grit behind at the bottom of the pot.

Baked Clams

MAKES 4 APPETIZER SERVINGS

Here's a recipe for juicy clams topped with crisp crumbs that has been served at Patsy's since the first day that Grandpa opened the doors. Scognamillo family lore says that these were the first seafood that I ever ate. (I can't argue with my mother's memory, although I bet it was fried calamari.) Even though these are called baked, they are really broiled. Unless you have someone in your life who is an experienced clam shucker, buy the clams on the half shell the day you plan to cook them.

24 Littleneck clams, shucked with the meat on the half shell

Salt and freshly ground black pepper

2 cups Seasoned Bread Crumbs (page 14)

¼ cup olive oil, for drizzling

2 lemons, cut into wedges

1. Position a rack about 8 inches from the heat source and preheat the broiler on high.

2. Season the clams very lightly with salt and pepper. Spoon the bread crumbs into the shells and smooth with the back of a spoon. Arrange the stuffed clam shells in a single layer in a broiler pan. Drizzle lightly with the olive oil to moisten the crumbs.

3. Broil until the bread crumbs are lightly browned, 2 to 3 minutes. Serve hot with the lemon wedges.

"The food at Patsy's is always so fresh and delicious. A great combo of the southern Italian food that we enjoy on our travels and the Italian-American cuisine of my New York childhood."
—Michael Kors

Mussels Marinara

MAKES 4 SERVINGS

Seafood in tomato sauce has a long history in Neapolitan cooking. In fact, marinara sauce is named for the mariners who supposedly created it. As mussels were plentiful and cheap in both Italy and America, my grandparents made this at home often. We serve it at the restaurant, too, usually over linguine as a pasta or main course. As an antipasto, serve it with crusty bread . . . but I didn't really have to tell you that, did I?

---

2 pounds cultivated mussels, such as Prince Edward Island (see Note, page 15)

2 cups cold water

2 cups Tomato Sauce (page 100)

2 tablespoons dry white wine

2 tablespoon chopped fresh flat-leaf parsley

Pinch of dried oregano

Salt and freshly ground black pepper

Sliced Italian bread, preferably toasted in a broiler or on a grill, for serving

1. Put the mussels in a large pot and add the water. Cover and bring to a boil over high heat. Cook just until the shells open, about 5 minutes. Using a slotted spoon, transfer the opened mussels to a colander, discarding any unopened mussels. Reserve the cooking liquid.

2. Line a wire strainer with moistened paper towels and set over medium bowl. Strain the cooking liquid through the strainer. Measure and reserve ½ cup of the strained liquid. (You can cool, cover, and freeze the remaining mussel cooking liquid for another use or as a fish stock.) Wash and dry the pot.

3. Bring the reserved cooking liquid, the tomato sauce, wine, parsley, and oregano to a boil over high heat. Cook, stirring often, until reduced to 2 cups, about 5 minutes. Add the mussels, cover, and cook until the mussels are reheated, about 3 minutes more. Season again with salt and pepper. Divide the mussels and sauce evenly among four soup bowls. Serve hot, with the toasted bread.

Mussels Marinara with Linguine

Use 3 cups Tomato Sauce, ¼ cup dry white wine, and ¾ cup cooking liquid. Boil for 5 minutes, or until reduced to about 3½ cups. Use as a sauce for 1 pound cooked linguine. Top each serving with mussels.

Shrimp Casino

We have customers who love our clams casino, but we also have some who don't like shellfish. This gives shrimp lovers a chance to enjoy the crispy topping on their favorite crustacean. This topping is very flavorful with extra helpings of bacon, pimientos, and Parmigiano.

24 colossal (U–15) shrimp, peeled, deveined, and butterflied

2 tablespoons olive oil, plus more for brushing

1 small yellow onion, chopped

Two 6.5–ounce jars pimientos, drained

8 slices bacon: 2 slices coarsely chopped, and 6 slices cut into 24 pieces

1/2 cup freshly grated Parmigiano–Reggiano cheese (about 2 ounces)

1 tablespoon chopped fresh flat–leaf parsley

1 tablespoon unsalted butter, at room temperature

Salt and freshly ground black pepper

1. Heat the oil in a medium skillet over medium heat. Add the onion and cook, stirring often, until lightly browned, about 4 minutes.

2. Transfer the onion to a food processor. Add the drained pimientos, chopped bacon, grated cheese, parsley, and butter and pulse until the bacon is finely chopped.

3. Position the broiler rack about 6 inches from the heat source and pre-heat the broiler on high. Lightly oil a broiler pan.

4. Arrange the shrimp, cut side down, with the tail sticking up, on the broiler pan. Spoon the pimiento mixture over the shrimp, dividing it equally. Broil until the exposed shrimp begins to turn opaque, about 1½ minutes. Remove the pan from the broiler. Season the shrimp with salt and pepper and top each with a piece of bacon. Return to the broiler and cook until the bacon is brown and crisp, about 2 minutes more. Serve hot.

Eggplant Caponata

MAKES 8 SERVINGS

My grandmother Concetta would start her array of antipasti with homemade eggplant caponata. Whenever I spread caponata on bread, I can't help but think of those days in Queens. When I make it now, I roast the eggplants, a change from the traditional frying method. Some people serve caponata chilled, but our family prefers it warm.

2 medium eggplants (about 1 pound each), trimmed, cut into ½-inch cubes

Olive oil, as needed

2 cups Tomato Sauce (page 100)

½ cup coarsely chopped pitted kalamata olives

8 anchovy fillets in oil, finely chopped

2 tablespoons drained nonpareil capers, rinsed

½ cup freshly grated Parmigiano-Reggiano cheese (about 2 ounces)

⅓ cup plain dried bread crumbs

1 tablespoon chopped fresh flat-leaf parsley

Salt and freshly ground black pepper

1 loaf Italian bread, sliced and toasted in a broiler or on the grill

1. Position two racks in the oven and preheat the oven to 450°F.

2. Spread the eggplant on 2 large rimmed baking sheets. Drizzle and toss the eggplant with oil to coat evenly. Roast, occasionally turning the eggplant, until the cubes are tender and golden brown, about 25 minutes.

3. Bring the tomato sauce to a boil in a large saucepan over high heat. Stir in the olives, anchovies, and capers. Reduce the heat to medium and simmer, uncovered, to blend the flavors for 2 to 3 minutes. Stir in the eggplant and simmer for 2 minutes more.

4. Transfer the eggplant mixture to a large bowl. Stir in the cheese, bread crumbs, and parsley. Season to taste with salt and pepper.

5. Serve warm, spreading the caponata on the toasted bread.

Eggplant Bruschetta

MAKES 4 TO 6 SERVINGS

The original bruschetta started with a slice of toasted bread, topped with juicy tomatoes. My version uses sliced eggplant instead of the bread. You'll love this twist on the old favorite.

TOPPING

2 tablespoons balsamic vinegar

2 garlic cloves, crushed through a press

1/3 cup plus 1 tablespoon extra-virgin olive oil

1 pound ripe plum tomatoes, coarsely chopped

4 scallions (white and green parts), thinly sliced

Salt and freshly ground black pepper

1/4 cup chopped fresh basil

1/2 cup all-purpose flour

3 large eggs

1 1/2 cups plain dried bread crumbs

1 medium globe eggplant (about 1 1/4 pounds), trimmed, peeled, and cut into 12 rounds about 1/2 inch thick

3/4 cup olive oil, or as needed, for frying

1. To make the topping: Whisk the vinegar and garlic together in a large bowl. Gradually whisk in the extra-virgin olive oil. Add the tomatoes and scallions and mix gently. Season to taste with salt and pepper. Cover and let stand at room temperature for at least 1 and up to 3 hours to blend the flavors. Just before serving, stir in the basil.

2. Spread the flour on a large plate. Beat the eggs together in a shallow bowl. Spread the bread crumbs on a second large plate. One at a time, coat an eggplant round with flour, dip in the eggs, and coat with the bread crumbs. Shake to remove excess coating and set on a baking sheet.

3. Preheat the oven to 200°F. Line a baking sheet with a wire cooling rack and place near the stove.

4. Heat the olive oil in a large nonstick skillet over medium-high heat until the oil is shimmering. Working in batches without crowding, add the eggplant (it should bubble up immediately) and fry, turning halfway through the cooking, until golden brown, about 3 minutes. Using a slotted spatula, transfer the eggplant slices to the rack and keep warm in the oven. If needed, add more oil to the skillet and reheat until shimmering before adding more eggplant.

5. For each serving, place 2 or 3 eggplant rounds on a dinner plate. Using a slotted spoon, top each with a generous amount of the tomato mixture. Serve immediately.

Eggplant Rollatini

MAKES 4 TO 6 SERVINGS

These are a specialty of my mom Rose. She learned them from my grandparents, who served them on the original menu as eggplant involtini, the Italian word for "roulades" (stuffed and rolled food). Rollatini is an entirely American word. Call them what you wish, they are wonderful, especially when made with love by my mom for one of our family get-togethers.

1 small globe eggplant (about 1 pound), trimmed, peeled, halved lengthwise and cut into ⅓-inch half-moons

⅓ cup all-purpose flour

4 large eggs

¾ cup olive oil, as needed

Salt and freshly ground black pepper

2 cups shredded fresh mozzarella cheese (about 8 ounces)

1 cup ricotta cheese

⅔ cup plus 3 tablespoons freshly grated Parmigiano-Reggiano cheese (about 3 ounces)

3 cups Tomato Sauce (page 100)

1. Cut the eggplant in half lengthwise. Cut each half into ⅓-inch-thick slices.

2. Spread the flour on a wide plate. Beat 3 of the eggs in a shallow bowl. Place the plate and bowl near the stove.

3. Line a large baking sheet with paper towels and place near the stove. Heat the oil in a large nonstick skillet over medium-high heat until the oil is shimmering. Working in batches, dip the eggplant into the flour, coat with the egg, and add to the oil. Cook, turning occasionally, until the eggplant is lightly browned, about 5 minutes. Using a slotted spatula, transfer the eggplant to the paper towels. Season to taste with salt and pepper.

4. Beat the remaining egg in a medium bowl. Add the mozzarella, ricotta, and ⅔ cup of the Parmigiano-Reggiano cheese and mix to combine.

5. Preheat the oven to 375 ° Lightly oil a 10 by 15-inch baking dish.

6. For each involtini, place a heaping tablespoon of the cheese mixture on the short end of an eggplant slice, roll it up, and place smooth side up in the dish. Pour the tomato sauce on top and sprinkle with the remaining 3 tablespoons Parmigiano cheese.

7. Bake until the sauce is simmering and the cheese has melted, about 20 minutes.

Bruschetta with Baked Figs and Gorgonzola

MAKES 6 SERVINGS

I am crazy about figs, and when they are in season, I eat them every which way. In fact, my father-in-law, Pete, grows figs, so I get them right off the tree. This combination of sweet figs and sharp gorgonzola, accented with the unique flavor of balsamic vinegar, will have you coming back for more, too. Here, I serve them on toast as a bruschetta, but they are also good as a topping for greens tossed with a balsamic vinaigrette.

Extra-virgin olive oil, as needed

²/₃ cup balsamic vinegar

2 teaspoons granulated sugar

12 ripe Black Mission figs, ends trimmed, cut in half lengthwise

1 cup crumbled Gorgonzola cheese (about 4 ounces)

12 slices baguette, toasted in a broiler or on a grill

¹/₄ cup fresh basil chiffonade, for garnish (see page 8)

1. Preheat the oven to 325°F. Lightly oil a baking dish suitable for serving that is large enough to hold the figs in a single layer.

2. Bring the vinegar and sugar in a small saucepan over high heat. Reduce the heat to medium and simmer briskly until the liquid has reduced by half, about 2 minutes. Set the reduction aside.

3. Meanwhile, arrange the figs in the baking dish, cut sides up. Brush with oil. Top each fig half with a heaping tablespoon of Gorgonzola. Bake until the cheese has melted, about 3 minutes.

4. Arrange the toasted baguette slices on a platter. Top each slice with a fig. Drizzle with the balsamic reduction and a little more oil. Sprinkle with the basil. Serve warm.

Salads and Soups

─⟨⟨⟩⟩─

Tre Colore Salad

Insalata di Frutti di Mare

Joe's Steak Salad

Three Bean Soup

Italian Wedding Soup

Pasta Fagioli

Peas and Macaroni Soup

Chicken Stock

Pavese Soup

Tre Colore Salad

MAKES 4 SERVINGS

We served a salad of white Belgian endive and green arugula before it was fashionable, although the red radicchio is a fairly new addition. I think their slight bitterness makes a great appetite teaser. Sinatra agreed with me. I remember one time when he convinced an entire table of people that arugula is really green radish tops. (I grant you that they look and taste a lot alike, but Frank was only kidding.)

VINAIGRETTE

¼ cup balsamic vinegar

1 garlic clove, minced

1 tablespoon finely chopped fresh basil

¾ cup extra-virgin olive oil

Salt and freshly ground black pepper

One 5-ounce bag baby arugula

½ small head radicchio, trimmed and coarsely chopped

1 large Belgian endive, stem trimmed and outer layer discarded, cut crosswise into ¼-inch-thick slices

Salt and freshly ground black pepper

A chunk of Parmigiano-Reggiano cheese, for shaving curls

1. To make the vinaigrette: Whisk the balsamic vinegar, garlic, and basil together in a small bowl. Gradually whisk in the oil. Season to taste with salt and pepper.

2. Toss the arugula, radicchio and endive together in a large bowl. Add ⅓ cup of the vinaigrette and toss again. (Leftover vinaigrette can be stored in a covered jar for up to 2 days. Let come to room temperature and shake well before using.) Season the salad to taste with salt and pepper.

3. Using a swivel-bladed vegetable peeler, shave a couple of ounces worth of curls from the block of cheese over the salad. Serve immediately.

Insalata di Frutti di Mare

MAKES 8 APPETIZER SERVINGS

One of the best non-vegetable salads around, this mixed seafood salad is often served as an appetizer, but more and more, people are ordering it as a main course salad—it is a fantastic lunch, especially during a hot New York summer. It doesn't matter what seafood you use, so use more of your favorites, or even add cooked and shelled clams or mussels. One hint, though: Don't marinate the salad too long or the vinaigrette will "cook" and toughen the seafood. To accomplish this, have all of the seafood prepared and chilled and mix it just before serving. You can also serve this as part of a Seven Fishes Feast for Christmas Eve.

1 pound calamari, cleaned and cut into ¹/₂-inch rings

8 jumbo (21/25 count) shrimp, peeled and deveined

¹/₃ cup plus 1 tablespoon fresh lemon juice

4 garlic cloves, minced

¹/₄ cup fresh basil chiffonade

³/₄ cup extra-virgin olive oil

Salt and freshly ground black pepper

1¹/₂ pounds octopus, cooked (**see** page 95), chilled, and cut into bite-size pieces

One 29-ounce can ready-to-eat scungilli, drained, rinsed, and chilled

12 cherry tomatoes, halved

4 celery ribs, cut into ¹/₂-inch dice

24 pitted kalamata olives, coarsely chopped

1. Bring a large saucepan of salted water to a boil over high heat. Add the calamari and reduce the heat to medium-low. Simmer for about 25 minutes or until tender. Using a wire strainer, transfer the calamari to a large bowl of iced water.

2. Add the shrimp to the water and cook just until they turn opaque and firm, about 4 minutes. Drain in a colander and transfer to the bowl with the calamari. Let stand until they cool, about 15 minutes. Drain again and pat dry with paper towels.

3. Whisk the lemon juice, garlic, and basil in a large bowl. Gradually whisk in the oil. Add the cooled calamari and shrimp with the octopus, scungilli, tomatoes, celery, and olives. Mix well. Season with salt and pepper to taste. Cover and refrigerate until lightly chilled, about 30 minutes. Serve cold.

Joe's Steak Salad

This is a great recipe if you follow our family's mantra never to waste food. It was my dad Joe who started marinating leftover steak for lunch, and ever since a customer saw him eating this, we have had it on the menu as a daily special. To this day, if Joe orders prime rib at another restaurant (an item that we don't serve at Patsy's and have to go out for), he will bring the leftovers home for this salad. You can grill the steak, but we like it pan-cooked just as much.

2 tablespoons balsamic vinegar

$1/2$ teaspoon salt

$1/4$ teaspoon freshly ground black pepper

$1/3$ cup plus 1 tablespoon extra-virgin olive oil

Two 12- to 14-ounce sirloin steaks, cut about 1 inch thick

2 scallions (white and green parts), thinly sliced

$1/4$ cup fresh basil chiffonade (see page 8)

2 garlic cloves, thinly sliced

One 5-ounce bag baby arugula

2 plum tomatoes, cut into $1/2$-inch rounds

1. Whisk the balsamic vinegar, salt, and pepper in a small bowl. Gradually whisk in the oil. Put the steaks in a glass baking dish just large enough to hold them and brush with about 3 tablespoons of the vinaigrette. Let stand at room temperature to lose their chill for about 15 minutes.

2. Heat a large skillet, preferably cast iron, over high heat until very hot. Turn on the kitchen exhaust fan. Add the steaks, shaking off the excess marinade, and cook until the undersides are nicely browned, about 4 minutes. Turn and cook until the other sides are browned and the steaks feel slightly resilient when pressed in the center, about 3 minutes more for medium-rare. Transfer the steaks to a carving board and let stand for 5 minutes. Wash and dry the baking dish.

3. Cut the steaks on a slight diagonal into ½-inch-thick slices. Arrange the steak in a single layer, overlapping as needed, in the baking dish. Sprinkle with the remaining vinaigrette. and top with the scallions, basil, and garlic. Season to taste with salt and pepper. Cover loosely and refrigerate for at least 15 minutes and up to 30 minutes (no longer!).

4. Divide the arugula and tomatoes evenly among four dinner plates. Top each with the steak slices. Drizzle with the vinaigrette and serve.

Three Bean Soup

Beans are inexpensive sources of protein and they fill you up. And somehow, they warm you up, too. This is a soup for one of those blustery winter days when the wind rips up West Fifty-sixth Street from the Hudson River. And because it uses canned beans, it can be ready to serve fairly quickly.

8 ounces small pasta shells or any small pasta for soup

¼ cup olive oil

4 ounces ¼-inch dice pancetta

1 medium yellow onion, chopped

2 garlic cloves, finely chopped

4 cups Chicken Stock (page 37) or reduced-sodium store-bought chicken broth

4 cups cold water

One 15-ounce can cannellini (white kidney) beans, drained and rinsed

One 15-ounce can pink beans, drained and rinsed

One 15-ounce can red kidney beans, drained and rinsed

2 sprigs fresh rosemary

2 scallions (white and green parts), finely chopped

¼ cup chopped fresh basil

Salt and freshly ground black pepper

1. Bring a large saucepan of salted water to a boil over high heat. Add the pasta and cook according to the package directions until tender. Drain well.

2. Meanwhile, heat the oil in a soup pot over medium heat. Add the pancetta and cook, stirring occasionally, until it begins to brown, about 5 minutes. Add the onion and garlic and cook, stirring occasionally, until the onion begins to brown, about 4 minutes.

3. Add the stock, water, beans, and rosemary. Bring to a boil over high heat. Reduce the heat to medium-low, cover, and simmer to blend the flavors for 15 minutes.

4. Discard the rosemary sprigs. Stir in the scallions, basil, and cooked pasta. Cover and simmer just until the pasta is heated through, about 2 minutes. Season to taste with salt and pepper.

Italian Wedding Soup

MAKES 14 TO 18 SERVINGS

I always thought that the name meant it was served at weddings, but actually it refers to the marriage of meat and vegetables in the soup. This makes a huge amount of soup, so bring out your biggest pot and make room in the freezer for leftovers.

6 ounces sweet Italian pork sausage

⅓ cup olive oil

2 medium yellow onions, chopped

3 garlic cloves, minced

7 cups reduced-sodium chicken broth

8 ounces sweet sopressata

8 ounces hot sopressata

1 head Savoy cabbage, cored

1 head escarole, rinsed

12 ounces broccoli florets

12 ounces leaf spinach

6 dried bay leaves

½ recipe Meatball-tini (page 13)

Salt and freshly ground black pepper

1. Position a broiler rack 6 inches from the heat source and preheat the broiler on high. Pierce the sausages a few times with a fork. Broil the sausages, turning occasionally, until browned on all sides. Let cool. Slice crosswise into ½-inch rounds.

2. Meanwhile, heat the oil in a very large stockpot over medium heat. Add the onions and garlic and cook until lightly browned, about 4 minutes. Add the broth, 6 quarts water, and sopressata to the pot. Bring to a boil over high heat. Reduce the heat to medium-low, cover, and simmer until well flavored, about 45 minutes.

3. Discard the casings from the sweet and hot sopressata, and cut the sopressata in ½-inch rounds.

4. Cut the cabbage into 1-inch pieces. Coarsely chop the escarole and spinach leaves. Add the sliced sausage, cabbage, escarole, broccoli, spinach, and bay leaves. Return to a boil over high heat. Reduce the heat to medium-low, cover, and simmer until the cabbage is tender, about 25 minutes. Add the meatballs and simmer until heated through.

5. Discard the bay leaves. Season to taste with salt and pepper. Ladle into bowls and serve hot.

Pasta Fagioli

MAKES 6 SERVINGS

Italian cooks know how to stretch their money. I was told that this wonderful bean and macaroni soup uses short pasta because the broken bits of the long varieties were sold at bargain prices. Everyone knows this by its name in Neapolitan dialect, pronounced "pasta faz-ool." Years ago, a couple of regular customers returned from a trip to Italy and were excited to tell us about a great soup they had eaten called "pahs-tah fah-gee-oh-lee," which is the textbook pronunciation. Nobody knew what the heck they were talking about until we wrote it down on paper.

8 ounces small pasta shells or any small pasta for soup

¼ cup olive oil

1 cup coarsely chopped yellow onions

1 garlic clove, minced

3 cups Tomato Sauce (page 100)

2 cups Chicken Stock (page 37) or reduced-sodium store-bought chicken broth

One 15-ounce can cannellini (white kidney) beans, drained and rinsed

1 tablespoon finely chopped fresh flat-leaf parsley

Salt and freshly ground black pepper

1. Bring a large pot of salted water to a boil over high heat. Add the shells and cook according to the package directions until tender. Drain and set aside.

2. Meanwhile, heat the oil in a large saucepan over medium heat. Add the onions and garlic and cook, stirring occasionally, until lightly browned, about 4 minutes.

3. Stir in the tomato sauce, stock, and beans and bring to a boil. Reduce heat to medium-low and cover. Simmer to blend the flavors, about 4 minutes.

4. Stir in the cooked pasta and parsley and cook just until the pasta is heated through, about 2 minutes. Season to taste with salt and pepper. Serve hot.

Peas and Macaroni Soup

MAKES 6 SERVINGS

My Aunt Anna loved this soup. If your kitchen is reasonably well stocked (and in most Italian American kitchens, prosciutto is a staple), then you can make this soup in a few minutes. But, she also did a variation with lots more pasta (usually broken linguine) cooked for about 30 minutes or so until the pasta was very thick and soft.

---

4 ounces small soup for pasta, such as tubetti or small shells

½ cup extra-virgin olive oil

1 medium yellow onion, finely chopped

2 medium scallions, white and green parts finely chopped

½ cup ¼-inch dice prosciutto

4 cups Chicken Stock (page 37) or reduced-sodium store-bought chicken broth

2 cups fresh or frozen peas

Salt and freshly ground black pepper

1. Bring a medium saucepan of salted water to a boil over high heat. Add the pasta and cook according to the package directions until al dente. Drain well.

2. Meanwhile, heat the oil in a large saucepan over medium heat. Add the onion and scallions and cook, stirring occasionally, until softened, about 3 minutes. Add the prosciutto and cook, stirring often, until its fat is translucent, about 5 minutes.

3. Add the stock, peas, and pasta and bring to a boil. Reduce the heat to medium-low and partially cover the pot. Simmer until the soup is thick and the pasta is soft, about 15 minutes. Season to taste with salt and pepper. Ladle into bowls and serve hot.

Chicken Stock

MAKES ABOUT 3 QUARTS

My grandfather never would have used canned chicken broth, and we make our stock from scratch. But I wonder if he tried some of the canned broths today if he would feel the same way, so feel free to use your favorite reduced-sodium brand in these recipes, if you wish. Here's how to make a big batch of chicken broth—make room in the freezer for a couple of quarts.

3 pounds chicken backs and wings

3 tablespoons vegetable oil

1 medium yellow onion, coarsely chopped

1 medium carrot, coarsely chopped

1 medium celery rib, coarsely chopped

2 dried bay leaves

5 whole black peppercorns

Salt

1. Preheat the oven to 450°F.

2. Toss the chicken backs and wings with the oil in a very large metal roasting pan. Roast for 20 minutes. Turn the chicken over and continue roasting until the chicken is well browned, about 15 minutes more.

3. Transfer the chicken to a large pot. Drain off the fat from the roasting pan and place the pan over medium heat. When the pan is sizzling, pour in water and bring to a boil, scraping up the browned bits in the pan with a wooden spoon. Pour into the pot. Add the onion, carrot, and celery. Add enough cold water to cover the mixture by 1 inch.

4. Bring to a boil over high heat, skimming off the foam that rises to the surface. Add the bay leaves and peppercorns. Reduce the heat to low. Simmer, uncovered, until the stock is well flavored, at least 2 and up to 4 hours.

5. Strain the stock through a large sieve into a large bowl: discard the solids. Let the stock cool until tepid. (If you want to speed this along, place the bowl in a large pan and surround the bowl with ice water. Skim off any yellow that that rises to the surface. Use immediately, or cool, cover, and refrigerate. (The stock can be refrigerated for up to 3 days or frozen in airtight containers for up to 3 months.)

Pavese Soup

MAKES 4 SERVINGS

I have no idea why this soup is named after Pavia, a town in Northern Italy. Are they known for eggs? I wonder, because this soup was originally served with a poached egg, although now we serve it with a fried egg, which is much easier. This is the kind of meal that Patsy would make after a long night at the restaurant, with ingredients he had on hand. This soup is best cooked with homemade broth.

4 thick-cut (½-inch) slices Italian bread, toasted

6 cups Chicken Stock (page 37) or reduced-sodium store-bought chicken broth

Salt and freshly ground black pepper

3 tablespoons olive oil (not extra-virgin)

4 large eggs

4 tablespoons Tomato Sauce (page 100)

Chopped fresh flat-leaf parsley, for sprinkling

Freshly grated Parmigiano-Reggiano cheese, for sprinkling

1. Place a slice of bread in each soup bowl.

2. Bring the stock to a boil in a medium saucepan over high heat. Season to taste with salt and pepper. Reduce the heat to low and keep warm.

3. Meanwhile, heat the oil in a large skillet over medium heat. Working in batches, crack the eggs into the skillet and cook, spooning the oil over the whites, just until the whites are set, about 1 minute. Using a slotted spoon, transfer each egg to a bowl and place on the bread.

4. For each serving, ladle about 1½ cups of stock around the egg-topped bread. Dot 1 tablespoon of tomato sauce over the egg. Sprinkle with the parsley and grated cheese. Serve hot.

Red Meat

❈

Beef Braciole

Italian Beef Stew

Steak Oreganata

Veal Scaloppini Besciamella

Veal Scaloppini Fra Diavolo

Veal Scaloppini à la Patsy

Stuffed Veal Spiedini

Osso Bucco

Pork Chop Siciliano

Quick Brown Sauce

Pork Meat Loaves

Pork Rollatini

Sweet Sausage Sliders

Liver Veneziana

Stewed Tripe à la Napolitana

Beef Braciole

MAKES 6 SERVINGS

Every Sunday, countless Italian American families serve beef braciole simmered in tomato sauce, sometimes adding sausage and meatballs to the pot. Back when we were closed on Mondays, we followed that tradition, just on a different day of the week. There is a marvelous marriage of flavors between the beef rolls and tomato sauce. At the restaurant, we serve very large braciole, and usually with rigatoni. Ever since my sister Tina was a little girl, these beef rolls have been her favorite meal.

STUFFING

4 slices firm white sandwich bread, torn into bite-size pieces

1 pound ground beef sirloin

1 large egg plus 1 large egg yolk, beaten together

1/3 cup seedless raisins

1/3 cup freshly grated Parmigiano-Reggiano cheese (about 1 1/2 ounces)

1/4 cup pine nuts

1 large garlic clove, minced

One 1 1/4-pound boneless top round beef roast (see Note), trimmed

Salt and freshly ground black pepper

6 large fresh basil leaves

1/2 cup all-purpose flour, for dredging

1. To make the stuffing: Soak the bread with about 1 cup cold water in a small bowl for 1 minute. Wring out the excess water, and transfer the soaked bread to a medium bowl. Add the ground sirloin, beaten egg and egg yolk, raisins, cheese, pine nuts, and garlic and mix well.

2. Using a thin sharp knife, cut the roast into 6 equal slices. One at a time, place a beef slice between two 1-gallon plastic storage bags. Using a flat meat pounder, pound the beef into a wide 5 by 8-inch piece of meat about 1/8 inch thick. Repeat with the remaining beef slices.

3. For each braciole, place a beef slice on the work surface, with the short side facing you. Season with salt and pepper. Place one-sixth (about 1/2 cup) of the stuffing near the bottom of the slice and top with a basil leaf. Starting at the bottom, roll up the beef to enclose the stuffing, tucking in the sides as you roll. Tie the beef at both ends with kitchen twine to secure the roll closed. Spread out the flour on a plate. Dredge the beef roll in the flour to coat and shake off the excess flour. Place on a baking sheet. (The rolls can be covered and refrigerated for up to 6 hours.)

4. Heat the oil in a large deep skillet or Dutch oven over medium-high heat until very hot but not smoking. Working in batches, without crowding, add the rolls and cook, turning occasionally, until browned all over, about 5 minutes. Return the rolls to the baking sheet.

5. Carefully discard the hot oil. Add the tomato sauce and wine to the

1 cup olive oil

6 cups Tomato Sauce
(page 100)

¼ cup dry white wine

1 pound rigatoni

Freshly grated
Parmigiano-Reggiano
cheese, for serving

skillet, mix well, and bring to a boil, stirring often. Arrange the rolls in the sauce and reduce the heat to low. Cover tightly and simmer, stirring occasionally, until the braciole are tender, 3 to 3½ hours, adding more water if the sauce becomes too thick. Transfer the beef to a carving board, tent with aluminum foil to keep warm, and let stand for 10 to 15 minutes while cooking the pasta. Keep the sauce warm over very low heat.

6. Meanwhile, about 20 minutes before serving, bring a large pot of salted water to a boil over high heat. Add the rigatoni to the boiling water and cook according to the package directions until al dente. Drain the pasta and transfer to a large serving bowl. Add 3 to 4 cups of the sauce to the rigatoni and mix well.

7. Remove the twine from the braciole. Cut each braciole in half lengthwise. Transfer to a deep serving platter and top with the remaining sauce. Serve hot, with the grated cheese passed on the side.

NOTE: Some butchers with Italian clientele have sliced top round specifically cut for braciole, and you can use it, if you wish. We make very large braciole, so you may have to overlap two slices to get the right size. Or you can buy a large beef round roast, cut off the braciole slices from the center of the roast, and use the remaining meat in pot roast or stew.

Italian Beef Stew

When I was growing up, we didn't have steak much, and my grandparents cooked with stew cuts like round and chuck. This is how I remember Patsy making it, with lots of vegetables to "beef up" the amount of meat in a rich sauce with wine and tomatoes, perfect for spooning over pasta.

1/2 cup olive oil

1/2 cup all-purpose flour

2 pounds boneless beef chuck, cut into 1 1/2-inch pieces

4 ounces 1/4-inch dice pancetta

2 medium yellow onions, chopped

4 medium celery ribs, cut into 1/2-inch dice

1 cup canned crushed tomatoes

1/2 cup dry white wine

1 cup water

1 pound baking potatoes, such as Russets, peeled and cut into 3/4-inch cubes

3 medium carrots, cut into 1/2-inch dice

1 cup thawed frozen peas

1/4 cup chopped fresh flat-leaf parsley

Salt and freshly ground black pepper

1. Heat the oil in a Dutch oven over medium-high heat. Spread out the flour on a large plate. Working in batches, coat the beef in the flour, shake off the excess flour and add to the Dutch oven. Cook, turning occasionally, until nicely browned, about 6 minutes. Transfer to a plate.

2. Add the pancetta to the Dutch oven and stir well. Add the onions and celery and cook, stirring occasionally, until lightly browned, about 5 minutes.

3. Stir in the tomatoes, wine, and 1 cup water and bring to a boil. Return the beef to the Dutch oven and cover tightly. Reduce the heat to medium-low. Simmer, stirring occasionally, until the meat is almost tender, about 2 hours.

4. Add the potatoes and carrots and cook until the beef and vegetables are tender, about 20 minutes more. Add the peas and cook until they are tender, about 7 minutes (about 3 minutes for thawed frozen peas). Stir in the parsley. Season to taste with salt and pepper. Serve hot.

Steak Oreganata

MAKES 2 TO 4 SERVINGS

There's nothing wrong with a plain steak. But this is Italian-style steak, topped with garlicky bread crumbs seasoned with some oregano. After all, oreganata means "flavored with oregano." You can serve one steak per person, or split the slices up among four people, making this a good dish to serve to kids or people with not-so-big appetites.

Two 12- to 14-ounce sirloin steaks, cut 1 inch thick

Olive oil, for coating and drizzling

1 teaspoon salt

$1/2$ teaspoon freshly ground black pepper

$3/4$ cup Seasoned Bread Crumbs (page 14)

Chopped fresh flat-leaf parsley, for garnish

1. Let the steaks stand at room temperature for 30 minutes. Brush both sides with the oil and season with the salt and pepper.

2. Position a broiler rack 6 inches from the heat source and preheat well. Lightly oil the broiler rack. Broil the steaks until the tops of the steaks are nicely browned, about 5 minutes. Turn the steaks and broil to brown the opposite sides, and until the steaks feel slightly resilient when pressed, 4 to 5 minutes more for medium-rare. Transfer to a carving board and let stand for 3 to 5 minutes.

3. Using a sharp knife, cut the steaks across the grain on a slight diagonal into $1/2$-inch-thick slices. Push the slices of each steak back together to resemble the original cut. Return to the broiler rack. Top each steak with an equal layer of bread crumbs and lightly drizzle with olive oil.

4. Return the steaks to the broiler and broil until the topping has browned, 1 to 2 minutes. Transfer the slices to dinner plates and serve.

Veal Scaloppini Besciamella

MAKES 4 SERVINGS

My grandfather called this dish by its French name, L'Ayolau, which was probably a restaurant that made a specialty of this dish. It is basically veal coated with a thick cream sauce (besciamella means "béchamel," which is the basic French white sauce), then crumbed and cooked. He loved it, and so do I. It's an indulgence, but live it up a little!

BESCIAMELLA

8 tablespoons (1 stick) unsalted butter

⅔ cup all-purpose flour

3 cups light cream or half-and-half, heated to steaming

2 tablespoons chopped fresh flat-leaf parsley

Salt and freshly ground black pepper

1¼ pounds veal scaloppini, cut into 8 pieces, pounded with a flat meat pounder to ⅛-inch thickness

⅔ cup all-purpose flour

1⅔ cups olive oil

5 large eggs, beaten to blend

3 cups plain dried bread crumbs

1. To make the besciamella: Melt the butter in a heavy-bottomed medium saucepan over medium heat. Sprinkle in the flour and whisk until smooth. Gradually whisk in the light cream and bring to a boil. Add the parsley and reduce the heat to medium-low. Simmer, whisking often, until the sauce is very thick and no raw flour taste remains, about 2 minutes. Season to taste with salt and pepper. Pour into a medium bowl. Press a sheet of plastic wrap directly on the surface to stop a skin from developing, and let cool to tepid. Refrigerate until completely cooled, at least 2 hours.

2. Meanwhile, heat ⅓ cup of the oil in a very large skillet over medium-high heat until hot but not smoking. Spread ⅓ cup of the flour on a large plate near the stove. Working in batches, coat the veal in the flour, shaking off the excess, and add to the skillet. Cook, turning once, until lightly browned, about 3 minutes. Transfer the veal to another plate. Let cool until tepid. Cover with plastic wrap and refrigerate until chilled, at least 1 hour.

3. Spread the remaining ⅓ cup flour on a plate. Put the besciamella sauce in another bowl. Beat the eggs in a wide shallow bowl. Spread the bread crumbs on a second plate. Pat each scaloppini with a paper towel to remove any moisture. Coat lightly in flour and shake off the excess. Now, using a small metal spatula, spread the veal on both sides with the sauce. Dip in the beaten eggs. Coat with the bread crumbs. Transfer to a large baking sheet.

4. Preheat the oven to 200°F. Place a wire cooling rack over a large rimmed baking sheet. Add the remaining 1⅓ cups oil to the skillet and heat over medium-high heat until the oil is shimmering but not smoking, or until a frying thermometer reads 350°F. Working in batches, add the scaloppini, and fry, turning once, until the coating is golden brown, about 2 minutes. Transfer to the wire rack and keep warm in the oven until all of the scaloppini are cooked. Serve hot.

Like in the Movies

A wise guy runs into Patsy's, being chased by an unknown assail-ant. He barricades himself in the men's room. Joe manages to talk him out of the restaurant, but not before a very dangerous, scary scene with him being threatened with a knife. Two days later, the man was found . . . after killing someone else with the same knife.

Veal Scaloppini Fra Diavolo

When you see Fra Diavolo, or "Brother Devil," on a menu, it means that it is devilishly spicy. (In Rome, the same treatment is called arrabiata, for "angry.") Our version is no exception, and gets its heat from both fresh cherry peppers and hot red pepper flakes. Of course, you can adjust the heat to taste by using sweet red peppers and less flakes.

2 pounds veal scaloppini, cut into 12 pieces, pounded with a flat meat pounder to $1/8$-inch thickness

$1/2$ cup all-purpose flour, for dredging

$1/3$ cup olive oil

3 cups Tomato Sauce (page 100)

1 cup Chicken Stock (page 37) or use reduced-sodium store-bought chicken broth

$1/4$ cup dry white wine

6 to 7 fresh or pickled hot cherry peppers (see Note), quartered, seeds removed

$1/4$ cup chopped fresh basil

$1/2$ teaspoon dried oregano

$1/2$ teaspoon hot red pepper flakes

Salt and freshly ground black pepper

1. Heat the oil in a very large skillet over medium-high heat until hot but not smoking. Spread the flour on a large plate near the stove. Working in batches, coat the veal in the flour, shaking off the excess, and add to the skillet. Cook, turning once, until lightly browned, about 4 minutes. Transfer the veal to a clean plate.

2. Carefully discard the oil from the skillet and wipe out the skillet with paper towels. Return the skillet to medium-high heat, add in the tomato sauce, stock, wine, cherry peppers, basil, oregano and red pepper flakes and stir to combine. Season to taste with salt and black pepper. Bring to a boil over high heat. Cook until the sauce has reduced by one-quarter, about 5 minutes. Return the veal to the skillet and reduce to medium-low. Cover and simmer until the sauce has thickened and the veal is opaque in the center when pierced with the tip of a sharp knife, about 3 minutes.

3. Transfer the veal and sauce to a platter and serve hot.

NOTE: Fresh hot cherry peppers (sometimes called cherry bomb peppers) are available in late summer at farmers' markets and Italian grocers. You can substitute 2 red jalapeño peppers, cut into rings and seeded, for the cherry peppers.

Veal Scaloppini à la Patsy

MAKES 4 SERVINGS

This was Grandma Concetta's favorite dish. It is a flavorful combination of particularly Italian ingredients—veal, prosciutto, mozzarella, and Marsala—melding together into an incredible meal. Serve a simple green vegetable on the side—steamed asparagus would be nice.

1/3 cup olive oil

1¼ pounds veal scaloppini, cut into 8 pieces, pounded with a flat meat pounder to 1/8-inch thickness

1/2 cup all-purpose flour

1 cup Chicken Stock (page 37)

1/2 cup Quick Brown Sauce (page 56)

1/3 cup dry Marsala wine

2 tablespoons unsalted butter

4 tablespoons chopped fresh flat-leaf parsley

Salt and freshly ground black pepper

8 slices (not paper-thin) prosciutto, cut into 5 by 3-inch pieces

8 thin slices fresh mozzarella cheese, cut into 5 by 3-inch pieces

1/4 cup freshly grated Parmigiano-Reggiano cheese (about 1 ounce)

1. Heat the oil in a very large skillet over medium-high heat until hot but not smoking. Spread the flour on a large plate near the stove. Working in batches, coat the veal in the flour, shaking off the excess, and add to the skillet. Cook, turning once, until lightly browned, about 4 minutes. Transfer the veal to another plate.

2. Meanwhile, position the broiler rack about 6 inches from the heat source and preheat the broiler on high.

3. Pour out the oil from the skillet, wipe out the skillet with paper towels, and return to medium-high heat. Add the stock, brown sauce, Marsala, butter, and 2 tablespoons of the parsley. Stir well and season to taste with salt and pepper. Place the veal in the sauce and bring to a boil. Cover, reduce the heat to medium-low and simmer, stirring often, until the sauce has thickened lightly and the veal looks opaque in the middle when pierced with the tip of a knife, about 3 minutes.

4. Spread out the scaloppini in the pan (they can overlap slightly), and top each with a piece of prosciutto, followed by a piece of mozzarella, and then sprinkle with Parmigiano cheese. Put the skillet in the broiler and broil until the mozzarella has melted, about 2 minutes.

5. Transfer the scaloppini to a serving platter and tent with aluminum foil. Boil the pan juices over high heat until they thicken slightly, about 2 minutes. Season to taste with salt and pepper. Pour over the scaloppini, sprinkle with the remaining parsley, and serve.

Stuffed Veal Spiedini

MAKES 4 SERVINGS

This is another family recipe that ended up on our menu after years of enjoying them at home. They come from my mother-in-law Josephine. Spiedini is the Italian name for kebabs, and are usually the typical marinated chunks of meat. In this case, scaloppini are stuffed with bread crumb and provolone filling, rolled, and skewered with bay leaves. Give them a try.

¼ cup olive oil, plus more for brushing

3 small yellow onions, 1 finely chopped and 2 cut lengthwise into sixths to make 12 wedges

3 cups Chicken Stock (page 37) or reduced-sodium store-bought chicken broth

12 dried bay leaves

1 cup boiling water

1 tablespoon tomato paste

1 tablespoon chopped fresh flat-leaf parsley

1 teaspoon salt

½ teaspoon freshly ground pepper

2 cups Seasoned Bread Crumbs (page 14)

2 pounds veal scaloppini, cut into 12 pieces, pounded with a flat meat pounder to ⅛-inch thickness

1. Heat the oil in a large saucepan over medium heat. Add the chopped onions and cook, stirring occasionally, until lightly browned, about 4 minutes. Add the stock and 8 of the bay leaves and bring to a boil. Reduce the heat to low and cover the saucepan. Simmer to infuse the stock with the bay leaves, about 12 minutes. At the same time, cover the remaining 4 bay leaves with boiling water in a small bowl and set aside to soak.

2. Whisk the tomato paste and parsley into the simmering stock. Season to taste with salt and pepper. Slowly whisk in 1 cup of the bread crumbs and mix until the mixture is thick enough to form a ball. Carefully remove bay leaves, rinse them under cold running water, and set aside. Cover and refrigerate the bread crumb mixture until cool, at least 30 minutes. Shape the mixture into 12 equal balls. Drain the water-soaked bay leaves.

3. Lightly oil a large rimmed baking sheet. Lightly season the scaloppini with the salt and pepper. For each veal roll, place a scaloppini on the work surface with a short side facing you. Place a bread crumb ball on the scaloppini and spread evenly to cover. Top with a scant 3 tablespoons of the provolone. Roll the scaloppini forward to make a tight packet, tucking in the sides as you roll to secure the filling. Transfer, seam side down, to the prepared baking sheet.

4. For each spiedini, on a metal grilling skewer, alternate 3 veal rolls, 3 onion wedges, and 3 bay leaves. Press the ingredients snugly together and

2 cups (8 ounces) shredded provolone cheese

SPECIAL EQUIPMENT

4 long metal grilling skewers (see Note)

return to the baking sheet. (The spiedini can be covered and refrigerated up to 2 hours before serving.)

5. Preheat the oven to 450°F.

6. Brush the veal spiedini with oil. Bake for 15 minutes. Turn, sprinkle generously with the remaining 1 cup bread crumbs, continue to bake until the bread-crumb topping has browned, about 8 minutes. Serve hot.

NOTE: Long metal skewers, at least 12 inches long, are best for grilling because they grip the meat much better than bamboo skewers. They are sturdy and reusable. Inexpensive metal skewers can be found at just about every supermarket, or look for fancier ones at kitchenware stores. If you must use bamboo skewers, you may want to use two, with a little space between them, for each spiedini and provide extra support. Soak the skewers in cold water for at least 30 minutes, then drain them before using. To keep the wood from burning, wrap the exposed ends in a small piece of aluminum foil as protection.

◆ Roasting Red Peppers ◆

Red peppers have a thick skin that is usually removed before eating. Roasting the peppers in the high heat of the broiler blisters the skin for easy peeling and cooks the peppers at the same time.

Position a broiler rack about 6 inches from the heat source and preheat the broiler on high. Broil the peppers, turning them occasionally, until the skin is blackened and blistered, 12 to 15 minutes. Do not burn through the pepper's flesh. Transfer the peppers to a paper bag and close the bag. Let them stand for 10 to 15 minutes until cool. Using a small knife, remove the skin, cut out the stems, and discard the seeds.

Osso Bucco

This rich and succulent veal stew is beloved by customers who know the truth of the proverb, "The sweetest meat is nearest the bone." And the bone marrow isn't so bad, either! Everyone at Patsy's remembers the time a customer ordered what he thought was his favorite veal dish. When this big chunk of meat arrived instead of delicate veal cutlets, the guy complained, "He forgot to take the bone out of my veal!" It was a case when another ancient adage, "The customer is always right," was hard to practice. Serve this with the Roasted Rosemary Potatoes page 145.

4 veal shanks, (1 to 1¼ pounds each)

½ cup all-purpose flour

½ cup olive oil

1 large yellow onion, chopped

6 medium celery ribs, cut into ½-inch dice

4 medium carrots, cut into ½-inch dice

1 cup Tomato Sauce (page 100)

½ cup hearty red wine

¾ cup chopped fresh basil

1. Preheat the oven to 350°F.

2. Lightly dust the shanks all over with flour, shaking off the excess. Heat the oil in a large deep skillet over medium-high heat until shimmering. Add the shanks and cook, turning occasionally, until well browned on all sides, about 10 minutes. Transfer the veal shanks to a roasting pan.

3. Drain all but ¼ cup of oil from the skillet and return to medium heat. Add the onion, celery, and carrots. Cook, stirring often, until the vegetables soften, 6 to 7 minutes. Stir in the tomato sauce, wine, and ½ cup of the basil and bring to a boil. Pour the vegetable mixture over the shanks.

4. Add water to the roasting pan until it reaches about halfway up the shanks. Cook, uncovered, turning the veal every 30 minutes, and adding hot water as needed to maintain the water level, until the veal is tender when pierced with the tip of a knife, 2½ to 3 hours. Transfer the shanks to a platter and tent with aluminum foil to keep warm.

5. Place the roasting pan over high heat and bring the cooking juices to a boil. Cook, stirring often, until it has reduced by one-quarter, about 10 minutes. Season to taste with salt and pepper.

6. For each serving, place a veal shank in a deep soup bowl. Spoon the pan juices on top and sprinkle with the remaining ¼ cup basil. Serve hot.

Pork Chop Siciliano

Many old Sicilian recipes use vinegar as a seasoning, knowing that its acidity can perk up a sauce. This is another dish that we have featured on the menu since 1944. It was originally made with red wine vinegar, but we recently switched over to balsamic, and that little adjustment took a good thing and made it even better.

4 center–cut rib pork chops (12 to 14 ounces each), cut 1¹/₂ inches thick

4 tablespoon extra–virgin olive oil

8 garlic cloves, thinly sliced

¹/₂ cup Chicken Stock (page 37) or use reduced–sodium store–bought chicken broth

¹/₂ cup Quick Brown Sauce (page 56)

¹/₄ cup chopped fresh basil

2 tablespoons balsamic vinegar

1 teaspoon finely minced fresh rosemary

Salt and freshly ground black pepper

1. Preheat the oven to 500°F.

2. Brush the chops on both sides with 2 tablespoons of the oil. Place them in a large ovenproof skillet. Roast for 12 minutes. Turn the chops over and continue roasting until they are browned and an instant-read thermometer, inserted horizontally into the center of a chop, reads 145°F, about 8 minutes. Remove the skillet and chops from the oven. Transfer the chops to a platter.

3. Meanwhile, add the remaining 2 tablespoons oil and the garlic to the skillet and warm over medium heat, stirring often, just until golden, 1 to 2 minutes. Stir in the stock, brown sauce, basil, vinegar, and rosemary, and season to taste with salt and pepper. Bring to a boil. Add the pork chops, reduce the heat to medium-low, and cover the skillet. Simmer just to blend the flavors, about 3 minutes.

4. Place each pork chop on a dinner plate and spoon the sauce over the chops, dividing it evenly.

◆ Quick Brown Sauce ◆

We use sauce in a few dishes for its flavor and to give body to a pan sauce. Classic brown sauce takes hours, but here's a quick version that works very well. Use a high-quality canned or aseptically packaged broth. For the tomato paste, which is a coloring more than a flavoring, use the variety in a tube, which is convenient because you don't have to open a whole can for half a teaspoon.

3 tablespoons unsalted butter

1 small yellow onion, chopped

One 13¾-ounce can reduced-sodium beef broth

2 tablespoons dry white wine or dry vermouth

½ teaspoon tomato paste

Pinch of dried thyme

1 small bay leaf

3 tablespoons all-purpose flour

Salt and freshly ground black pepper

1. Melt the butter in a small saucepan over medium heat. Add the onion and cook, stirring often, until browned, about 4 minutes. Stir in the flour. Gradually stir in the broth, followed by the wine, tomato paste, thyme, and bay leaf and bring to a simmer. Reduce the heat to low and simmer until thickened and slightly reduced, about 10 minutes.

2. Strain the sauce and discard the solids. Season to taste with salt and pepper. (The sauce can be cooled, covered, and refrigerated for 3 days. Or freeze the sauce in an airtight container for up to 2 months; thaw before using.)

Variation: Chicken Brown Sauce

Substitute reduced-sodium chicken broth or 1¾ cups Chicken Stock (page 37) for the beef broth.

Pork Meat Loaves

MAKES 6 TO 8 SERVINGS

My son Peter (who is an aspiring young chef) loves this meat loaf, which is in our rotation at home as one of our favorite dishes. It's one of those recipes that I just make off the top of my head. Flavor-wise, it blows regular beef meat loaf out of the water. I shape it into two small loaves because they cook faster than a single big loaf.

Olive oil, as needed

1/2 cup finely chopped white onion

1/4 cup plain dried bread crumbs, plus more as needed for the work surface

1/4 cup freshly grated Parmigiano-Reggiano cheese

2 large eggs, beaten

1 tablespoon Worcestershire sauce

1 tablespoon chopped fresh flat-leaf parsley

1 teaspoon salt

1/2 teaspoon ground pepper

2 pounds ground pork

4 ounces fresh mozzarella cheese cut into 1/2-inch cubes

1/2 cup fresh or thawed frozen peas

4 cups Tomato Sauce (page 100)

2 cups reduced-sodium chicken broth

1/4 cup dry white wine

1. Position a broiler rack about 8 inches from the heat source and preheat the broiler on high. Lightly oil a flameproof 10 by 15-inch baking dish.

2. Mix together the onion, bread crumbs, Parmigiano cheese, eggs, Worcestershire sauce, parsley, salt, and pepper in a large bowl. Add the pork and mix with your hands until well combined. Divide the mixture in half.

3. Dust a flat work surface with extra bread crumbs. Transfer half of the meat mixture to the work surface and shape into a 10 by 7-inch rectangle. Leaving a 2-inch border, scatter 1/2 cup of the mozzarella cubes and 1/4 cup of the peas into the center of the rectangle. Fold the meat mixture over the mozzarella and peas to enclose them, and shape into a thick loaf about 10 inches long. Transfer the meat loaf to the baking dish. Repeat with the remaining meat mixture, 1/2 cup mozzarella, and 1/4 cup peas. Brush the tops of the meat loaves with oil.

4. Broil the meat loaves until the tops are browned, 2 to 3 minutes. Remove from the broiler. Position a rack in the center of the oven and preheat the oven to 400°F.

5. Pour the tomato sauce, broth, and wine over the meat loaves. Cover the baking dish with aluminum foil. Bake until an instant-read thermometer inserted into the center of a loaf reads 160°F, about 40 minutes. Let stand for 10 minutes. Uncover the baking dish and slice the meat loaves. Serve hot, with the sauce on top.

Pork Rollatini

Succulent pork rolls filled with three cheeses are a popular specialty on our menu. They are pretty big, and while some guests can polish off two rollatini with no problem, people with smaller appetites will only want one . . . yet probably ask for seconds. Know your audience and make enough accordingly.

1 center-cut boneless pork loin roast (about 1¼ pounds), trimmed

1 cup finely chopped fresh mozzarella cheese (about 4 ounces)

¾ cup freshly grated Parmigiano-Reggiano cheese (about 3 ounces)

½ cup whole-milk ricotta cheese

2 large eggs, beaten to blend

⅓ cup finely chopped prosciutto

2 tablespoons unsalted butter, melted

8 slices bacon

1 tablespoon olive oil

½ cup Chicken Stock (page 37) or reduced-sodium store-bought chicken broth

⅓ cup dry white wine

⅓ cup finely minced shallots

Salt and freshly ground black pepper

1. Using a thin sharp knife, cut the loin into 8 equal slices about ⅓ inch thick. One at a time, place a pork slice between two 1-gallon plastic storage bags. Using a flat meat pounder, pound the pork into thin pieces 4 by 6 inches. Repeat with the remaining pork slices.

2. Preheat the oven to 450°F. Lightly oil a large ovenproof baking dish or casserole.

3. Mix together the mozzarella, Parmigiano, and ricotta cheeses, eggs, prosciutto, and butter in a medium bowl.

4. For each rollatini, place a pork slice on the work surface with a narrow end facing you. Spoon about one-eighth (about ¼ cup) of the cheese mixture near the bottom of the pork slice. Roll up the slice to enclose the filling, tucking in the ends as you roll. Wrap a bacon strip in a diagonal spiral around the pork slice. Arrange the rollatini in the baking dish.

5. Bake the rollatini for 8 minutes. Turn them over and bake until the bacon is browned and crisp, about 8 minutes more. Mix the broth, wine, and shallots together in a small bowl and season to taste with salt and pepper. Pour the broth mixture over the pork and continue baking until the liquid is hot, about 3 minutes. Let the rollatini stand about 5 minutes.

6. To serve, transfer the rollatini to a deep platter. Pour the pan juices on top and serve hot.

Sweet Sausage Sliders

MAKES 4

Miniature burgers go down easy, especially when they are made from sweet Italian sausage, topped with roasted red peppers and provolone cheese. We sell these by the truckload at Patsy's.

4 links sweet Italian pork sausage (each about 6 inches long)

4 tablespoons olive oil

Twelve 3–inch–square pieces Roasted Red Peppers (page 53)

Twelve 3–inch–square slices provolone cheese

1 garlic clove, minced

12 mini brioche buns, slider rolls, or small dinner rolls, split

Pitted green olives, for serving

1. Cut each sausage lengthwise, almost slicing in two, then spread the sausage out flat like an open book. Cut each sausage crosswise into thirds, giving you 12 pieces.

2. Heat 1 tablespoon of the oil in a large skillet over medium-high heat until hot but not smoking. Add the sausage, cut sides down, and cook, turning often, until browned on all sides and the sausage shows no sign of pink when pierced with the tip of a sharp knife, 7 to 8 minutes.

3. Turn off the heat, but leave the skillet on the burner. Top each piece of sausage with a slice of red pepper followed by a slice of provolone. Cover the skillet tightly and let the residual heat melt the cheese.

4. Meanwhile, position a rack in the broiler about 6 inches from the heat source and preheat the broiler on high.

5. While the broiler is preheating, heat the remaining 3 tablespoons oil with the garlic in a small saucepan over medium heat, stirring often, until the garlic is golden, about 2 minutes. Pour the garlic oil into a small bowl.

6. Brush the cut sides of the buns with the garlic oil. Place the buns, cut sides up, on the broiler rack. Broil until toasted, about 30 seconds.

7. For each slider, tuck a sausage portion in a bun. Spear a green olive on a wooden toothpick and poke it into the slider to hold it together. Serve hot.

Liver Veneziana

MAKES 4 TO 6 SERVINGS

Grandpa Patsy was fond of saying that liver Veneziana is the Italian version of sweet and sour pork. Venice has many traditional sweet and sour dishes, probably because of Middle Eastern cuisine's influence when the silk and spice routes were in full operation. I know many people who will only eat liver when it is cooked this way, smothered in vinegar-spiked onions.

²/₃ cup olive oil

2 medium yellow onions, cut into ¹/₈-inch-thick half-moons

1 cup Chicken Stock (page 37) or use reduced-sodium store-bought chicken broth

¹/₃ cup dry white wine

¹/₄ cup red wine vinegar

2 tablespoons unsalted butter

Salt and freshly ground black pepper

One 2¹/₄-pound calf's liver, rinsed and patted dry

¹/₂ cup all-purpose flour, for dredging

¹/₄ cup fresh basil chiffonade (see page 8)

1. Heat ⅓ cup of the olive oil in a large skillet over medium-high heat. Add the onions and cook, stirring occasionally, until they are very tender and caramelized, about 10 minutes.

2. Stir in the stock, wine, vinegar, and butter, and season to taste with salt and pepper and bring to a boil. Remove from the heat and cover to keep warm. Wash and dry the skillet.

3. Place the liver on the work surface with the long side facing you. Cut the liver vertically on a slight diagonal into ¼-inch-thick slices to yield approximately 24 pieces. Spread the flour on a plate. Coat the liver slices on both sides with flour, shaking off the excess.

4. Heat the remaining ⅓ cup oil in the skillet over medium-high heat until hot but not smoking. Working in batches without crowding, add the liver slices and cook, turning once, until browned on both sides but still quite pink inside when pierced with the tip of a sharp knife, 2 to 3 minutes. Transfer the liver slices to a platter.

5. Discard the oil from the skillet. Return the liver slices to the skillet and pour the onion mixture on top. Bring to a boil over medium-high heat. Reduce the heat to medium-low and simmer, uncovered, just until the liver is heated through, 1 to 2 minutes.

6. Transfer the liver slices and onions to a large platter and sprinkle with the basil. Serve hot.

Stewed Tripe à la Napolitana

MAKES 4 TO 6 SERVINGS

My dad Joe remembers being able to buy different kinds of tripe (each from one of the cow's four stomachs, plus lamb tripe), but now you can only get the honeycomb cut without a search. Burt Lancaster (who spoke perfect Italian, by the way), used to love our tripe, cooked in this Old World way. One night, a difficult woman customer was loudly arguing with Joe, with the accusation that the signed celebrity photos hanging on our wall were forgeries. Dad pointed across the room to Burt. That shut her up.

2 pounds beef honeycomb tripe

$\frac{1}{3}$ cup olive oil

2 medium yellow onions, cut into $\frac{1}{4}$–inch–thick half-moons

2 ounces $\frac{1}{8}$ inch sliced prosciutto, cut into thin slivers (about $\frac{2}{3}$ cup)

1 cups Tomato Sauce (page 100)

2 cups Chicken Stock (page 37) or use reduced-sodium store–bought chicken broth

$\frac{2}{3}$ cup dry white wine

1 cup fresh or thawed frozen peas

$\frac{1}{3}$ cup chopped fresh basil

2 tablespoons unsalted butter

Salt and freshly ground black pepper

1. Place the tripe in a large pot and add enough cold water to cover by about 2 inches. Bring to a boil over high heat. Reduce the heat to low and cover the pot. Simmer until the tripe is tender but still has some resistance, 2 to 2½ hours.

2. Drain the tripe, rinse under cold running water, and let cool. Slice the tripe into strips about 4 inches long and ½ inch wide.

3. Heat the oil in a large deep skillet over medium heat. Add the onions and cook, stirring occasionally, until lightly browned, 3 to 4 minutes. Stir in the prosciutto and cook for 1 minute. Stir in the tomato sauce, stock, wine, peas, basil, and butter, then add the tripe. Bring to a boil over medium-high heat. Reduce the heat to low, cover the pot, and simmer 8 to 10 minutes, adding a few tablespoons of additional water if the sauce gets too thick and the tripe sticks to the pot.

4. Season to taste with salt and pepper. Spoon into deep soup bowls and serve hot.

Poultry

—∞∞∞—

Anna's Chicken Gravy

Chicken and Mushroom Bianco

Roasted Chicken with Rosemary-Garlic Sauce

Chicken à la Vodka with Asparagus and Artichoke Hearts

Classic Chicken Cacciatore

Chicken Contadina with Sausage and Peppers

Chicken Pizzaiola

Chicken Breast with Prosciutto, Mushrooms, and Capers

Rose's Chicken Legs with Peas and Marsala

Anna's Chicken Gravy

MAKES 4 TO 6 SERVINGS

I remember many family meals where my aunt Anna would simmer chickens in tomato sauce to serve a hungry crowd of relatives. Part of the fun of serving this dish is carving the falling-apart chicken and licking the sauce off your fingers.

One 4-pound chicken

½ cup extra-virgin olive

1 medium yellow onion, sliced into thin half-moons

½ cup ¼-inch dice prosciutto

One 28-ounce can whole tomatoes in juice, undrained

2 tablespoons tomato paste

¼ cup dry white wine

¼ cup chopped fresh basil, plus a few whole leaves for garnish

Salt and freshly ground black pepper

1 pound perciatelli or bucatini

Freshly grated Parmigiano-Reggiano cheese, for serving

1. Heat the oil in a medium Dutch oven (preferably oval) over medium-high heat until the oil is hot but not smoking. Add the chicken and cook, turning occasionally, until browned on all sides, about 6 minutes. Transfer to a platter.

2. Reduce the heat to medium and add the onion and prosciutto. Cook, stirring occasionally, until the onion is tender and lightly browned, about 4 minutes.

3. Stir in the tomatoes with their juices, coarsely crushing the tomatoes between your fingers as they go into the pot. Stir in the wine and season to taste with salt and pepper. Return the chicken to the Dutch oven and bring to a boil over medium-high heat. The tomato sauce should come about two-thirds up the sides of the chicken; add water as needed. Reduce the heat to medium-low and cover tightly. Simmer, occasionally turning the chicken and stirring the sauce, until the chicken is very tender and shows no sign of pink when pierced at the thighbone, about 1¼ hours. During the last few minutes, stir in the basil. Carefully transfer the chicken to a carving board (it will probably be falling apart, but that's good!) and let stand for about 10 minutes.

4. Bring a large pot of salted water to a boil over high heat. Add the perciatelli and cook according to the package directions until al dente. Drain and return it to its cooking pot. Stir in half of the sauce and transfer to a large serving bowl. Carve the chicken and put the meat, remaining sauce, and whole basil leaves on the pasta.

Chicken and Mushroom Bianco

While the mainstay of our kitchen is a traditional red sauce, here is a great weeknight recipe for a "white" cacciatore with mushroom and herbs, but no tomatoes. Serve it over orzo, the rice-shaped pasta.

¼ cup olive oil

One 4-pound chicken, cut into 8 serving pieces

1 medium yellow onion, finely chopped

2 garlic cloves, minced

1½ pounds white button mushrooms, sliced

1 tablespoon finely chopped fresh rosemary, plus rosemary sprigs for garnish

Salt and freshly ground black pepper

½ cup dry white wine

1. Heat the oil in a large, deep skillet over medium-high heat. Working in batches, add the chicken and cook, turning occasionally, until browned on all sides, about 6 minutes. Transfer to a plate.

2. Add the onion to the fat in the skillet and cook, stirring often, until softened, about 3 minutes. Stir in the garlic and cook until fragrant, about 1 minute. In four additions, stir in the mushrooms and cook, stirring often, letting the first batch soften before adding the next, about 3 minutes. Add the wine and rosemary and bring to a boil, scraping up any browned bits in the pan with a wooden spoon. Season to taste with salt and pepper.

3. Return the chicken to the skillet. Reduce the heat to medium-low. Cover tightly and simmer until the chicken shows no sign of pink when pierced at the thighbone, about 45 minutes. Season again with salt and pepper. Transfer to a serving platter, top with the rosemary sprigs, and serve hot.

Roasted Chicken with Rosemary-Garlic Sauce

MAKES 4 SERVINGS

I love rosemary with chicken. This method of high roasting creates a golden crust and a flavorful light sauce. It will make some smoke in the oven, so turn on the exhaust fan before you get started. Use small chickens for even cooking.

Two 3½-pound chickens

¼ cup plus 2 tablespoons olive oil, plus more for the roasting pan

12 garlic cloves, halved

1 cup Chicken Brown Sauce (see Variation page 56)

¼ cup dry white wine

¼ cup balsamic vinegar

¼ cup chopped fresh basil

1 tablespoon chopped fresh rosemary

1 teaspoon dried oregano

1. Preheat the oven to 450°F. Lightly oil a large metal roasting pan.

2. Brush the chicken quarters generously with ¼ cup of the oil. Arrange the chicken quarters, skin side down, in the roasting pan.

3. Roast for 25 minutes. Turn the chicken quarters over, and roast for 15 minutes more.

4. Meanwhile, heat the remaining 2 tablespoons oil and the garlic together in a medium saucepan over medium heat and cook, stirring often, until the garlic is golden, about 2 minutes. Stir in the chicken brown sauce, wine, vinegar, basil, rosemary, and oregano. Season to taste with salt and pepper. Bring to a boil over high heat. Reduce the heat to low and simmer, uncovered, to combine the flavors, about 3 minutes. Set the sauce aside.

5. After the chicken has roasted for 40 minutes, pour off the excess fat from the roasting pan. Pour the sauce over the chicken in the pan and continue roasting until an instant-read thermometer inserted in the thickest part of the breast reads 165°F, about 5 minutes. Remove from the oven and let stand for 5 to 10 minutes.

6. Transfer the chicken to a large platter. Scrape the browned bits in the pan into the sauce, and pour the sauce over the chicken. Serve hot.

Chicken à la Vodka with Asparagus and Artichoke Hearts

MAKES 4 SERVINGS

When our jarred sauces debuted in 1994, I developed this recipe to show off our vodka sauce at supermarket demonstrations. Why didn't I cook pasta? Back then, few supermarkets had kitchens for cooking on premise. How times have changed. Needless to say, you can buy Patsy's jarred sauce for a very fast supper if you don't have time to make your own. And as good as this dish is, maybe it is just a little better served with rigatoni or rice to soak up the sauce.

1 pound fresh asparagus, woody ends snapped off, spears cut diagonally into 2-inch pieces

½ cup all-purpose flour

4 skinless, boneless chicken breast halves (about 6 ounces each), each sliced in half horizontally into scaloppini

¼ cup olive oil

3 cups Vodka Sauce (see page 122)

2 cups Chicken Stock (page 37) or reduced-sodium store-bought chicken broth

One 14-ounce can quartered artichoke hearts, drained and rinsed

Salt and freshly ground black pepper

1. Bring a large saucepan of lightly salted water to a boil over high heat. Add the asparagus and cook until crisp-tender, about 2 minutes. Drain, rinse under cold water, and drain again on paper towels.

2. Spread the flour on a plate. Coat the chicken in the flour, shake off the excess, and transfer the chicken to a clean plate.

3. Heat the olive oil in a large deep skillet over medium-high heat until the oil is shimmering but not smoking. Add the chicken and cook, turning once, until browned on both sides, about 6 minutes. Transfer to paper towels to drain.

4. Carefully pour off all but 1 tablespoon of oil from the skillet. Stir in the vodka sauce, stock, artichoke hearts, and reserved asparagus. Season to taste with salt and pepper. Return the chicken to the skillet and reduce the heat to medium-low. Cover and simmer until the chicken shows no sign of pink when pierced with the tip of a knife, about 6 minutes. Transfer the chicken to a platter and pour the sauce on top. Serve hot.

Classic Chicken Cacciatore

MAKES 4 SERVINGS

Here's the traditional recipe for chicken cacciatore, loaded with mushrooms. Did you know that cacciatore *means "hunter" in Italian? The original chicken cacciatore got its name because it featured wild mushrooms foraged from the forest.*

½ cup all-purpose flour

One 4-pound chicken, cut into 8 serving slices

¼ cup olive oil

10 ounces white button mushrooms, thinly sliced

1 small yellow onion, chopped

2 cups Tomato Sauce (page 100)

1½ cups Chicken Stock (page 37) or reduced-sodium store-bought chicken broth

¼ cup dry white wine

¼ cup dry Marsala

1 tablespoon unsalted butter

Salt and freshly ground black pepper

1. Spread the flour on a plate. Coat the chicken in the flour, shake off the excess, and put the chicken on a clean plate.

2. Heat the oil in a large deep skillet over medium-high heat. Working in batches, add the chicken and cook, turning occasionally, until browned on all sides, about 6 minutes. Transfer to a plate.

3. Pour off all but 2 tablespoons of the oil in the skillet and reduce the heat to medium. Add the mushrooms and onion and cook, stirring occasionally, until the mushrooms are lightly browned, about 5 minutes.

4. Add the tomato sauce, stock, wine, Marsala, and butter and bring to a boil. Season to taste with salt and pepper. Return the chicken to the skillet and reduce the heat to medium-low. Cover and simmer until the chicken shows no sign of pink when pierced with the tip of a sharp knife, 35 to 40 minutes. Transfer the chicken to a platter, top with the sauce, and serve hot.

Chicken Contadina with Sausage and Peppers

Here's a dish that has many variations, but we call the basic recipe contadina, which means "countryside" in Italian, because it is the perfect example of the kind of rustic cooking that we love. It doesn't have a sauce, just separately cooked potatoes, sausage, and vegetables brought together with a splash of broth and a sprinkle of parsley. For a spicy version, use hot sausage and substitute 8 fresh or pickled red cherry peppers, seeded and chopped, for the bell peppers. Without the potatoes, it is sometimes called scarpariello, which means "shoemaker-style," and could mean that dish that is "cobbled" together.

10 ounces sweet Italian pork sausage, 2–3 links, pierced with a fork

2 large baking potatoes, (about 1¼ pounds), peeled, and cut into ½-inch cubes (or use a melon baller to create the balls)

4 tablespoons olive oil, divided

2 chicken breast halves, with skin and bone (each about 12 ounces)

3 chicken thighs, with skin and bone (each about 5 ounces)

salt and freshly ground pepper

2 large red bell peppers, cored, seeded, and cut into ½-inch-wide strips

1. Position a broiler rack about 6 inches from the heat source and preheat the broiler on high. Broil the sausages, turning often, until browned and cooked through, 12 to 15 minutes. Transfer to a carving board and let cool. Cut crosswise into ½-inch rounds.

2. Preheat the oven to 450°F.

3. Using a heavy cleaver, chop the chicken breast halves and thighs through the bone into 2-inch chunks. (Or have the butcher do this at the market.) Season the chicken with 1 teaspoon salt and ½ teaspoon pepper. Heat 2 tablespoons of the oil in a large skillet over medium-high heat. In batches, add the chicken and cook, turning occasionally, until browned, about 5 minutes. Set aside.

4. On a large rimmed baking sheet, toss the potatoes with 2 tablespoons of the oil and spread in a single layer. Transfer the chicken to the baking sheet with the potatoes, and set the skillet with the pan juices aside. Roast, turning the potatoes and chicken occasionally, until the potatoes are tender and the chicken is cooked through with no sign of pink when pierced, about 20 minutes.

10 ounces white button mushrooms, thinly sliced

6 garlic cloves, minced

1/2 cup Chicken Stock (page 37) or reduced-sodium store-bought chicken broth

1/4 cup chopped fresh flat-leaf parsley

1/4 teaspoon dried oregano

5. Add the remaining 2 tablespoons oil in the skillet over medium-high heat. Add the red peppers and cook for 2 minutes. Add the mushrooms and cook, stirring often, until the mushrooms are lightly browned, about 6 minutes. Stir in the garlic and cook just until fragrant, about 1 minute.

6. Fold in the potatoes, sausage and chicken and mix well. Cook uncovered, stirring occasionally, until the sausage is heated through, about 2 minutes. Stir in the stock, parsley, and oregano and cook, scraping up the browned bits in the skillet with a wooden spoon, until the broth is absorbed and the ingredients are moistened, about 1 minute. Season to taste with salt and pepper. Serve hot.

I ♥ Patsy's

Joe was in the hospital and one customer in particular, a known "wise guy," was very worried and asked often about Joe's health. When Joe came back, the man sat him down at his table during a busy dinner service.

"How you feeling, Joe? You OK?"

"I'm fine. Just a little heart problem. I'm fixed now."

"You sure? You don't need a heart transplant or anything like that?"

"No, really. Why?"

"I was thinkin' . . . Pick out one of these strong, young guys. I'll rip his heart out and have it delivered to the hospital any time you need it."

We never knew if he was kidding or not.

Chicken Pizzaiola

Pizzaiola is the basic, all-purpose red sauce that is excellent with just about anything from steaks to pork chops, and sausages to veal. It is often no more than tomatoes and oregano. Our version is more substantial with mushrooms and red peppers. Here we pair it with chicken, and it is a winning combination.

½ cup all-purpose flour

4 skinless, boneless chicken breasts (about 6 ounces each), each sliced in half horizontally into scaloppini

½ cup olive oil

2 large red bell peppers, cored, seeded, and cut into ½-inch-wide strips

6 ounces white button mushrooms, sliced

4 cups Tomato Sauce (page 100)

1 cup Chicken Stock (page 37) or reduced-sodium store-bought chicken broth

¼ cup dry white wine

¼ cup chopped fresh flat-leaf parsley

½ teaspoon dried oregano

Salt and freshly ground black pepper

Freshly grated Parmigiano-Reggiano cheese, for serving

1. Spread the flour on a plate. Coat the chicken in the flour, shake off the excess, and transfer the chicken to a clean plate.

2. Heat the olive oil in a large deep skillet over medium-high heat until the oil is shimmering but not smoking. Add the chicken and cook, turning once, until lightly browned on both sides, about 4 minutes. Transfer to paper towels to drain.

3. Carefully pour off all but 2 tablespoons of the oil from the skillet. Return the skillet to medium heat. Add the red peppers and mushrooms and cook, stirring occasionally, until the mushrooms are lightly browned, about 5 minutes.

4. Stir in the tomato sauce, stock, wine, parsley, and oregano and bring to a boil. Season to taste with salt and black pepper. Return the chicken to the skillet. Reduce the heat to medium-low and cover tightly. Simmer until the chicken shows no sign of pink when pierced with the tip of a knife, about 5 minutes. Transfer the chicken to a platter and top with the sauce. Serve hot, with the grated cheese passed on the side.

Chicken Breast with Prosciutto, Mushrooms, and Capers

MAKES 4 SERVINGS

When someone doesn't know what to order, I point them towards this dish because it has so many Italian flavors in every bite. Earthy mushrooms, salty prosciutto, fragrant basil, and slightly bitter capers combine to make this luscious wine sauce.

4 boneless, skinless chicken breast halves (about 6 ounces each), each sliced in half horizontally into scaloppini

1/2 cup all-purpose flour

3 large eggs, beaten

1/4 cup olive oil

8 ounces fresh white button mushrooms, sliced

1/2 cup 1/8-inch-wide strips of prosciutto

1 1/4 cups Quick Brown Sauce (page 56)

1/3 cup fresh lemon juice

1/3 cup chopped fresh basil

1/3 cup dry white wine

2 tablespoons unsalted butter

2 tablespoons drained nonpareil capers, rinsed

Salt and freshly ground black pepper

1. Spread the flour on a plate. Beat the eggs in a shallow bowl. Place the flour and eggs near the stove.

2. Heat the oil in a large skillet over medium-high heat. Working in batches, add the chicken and cook, turning once, until lightly browned, about 4 minutes. Transfer the chicken to a clean plate.

3. Reduce the heat to medium. Add the mushrooms and prosciutto and cook, stirring occasionally, until the mushrooms are beginning to brown, about 5 minutes.

4. Add the sauce, wine, lemon juice, capers, and butter and bring to a boil. Season to taste with salt and pepper. Return the chicken to the skillet. Reduce the heat to medium-low and cover tightly. Simmer until the chicken shows no sign of pink when pierced with the tip of a sharp knife, about 5 minutes.

5. Transfer the chicken to a platter. Increase the heat to high and boil the sauce in the skillet, stirring often, until lightly thickened, about 3 minutes. Spoon the sauce on top of the chicken. Serve hot.

Rose's Chicken Legs with Peas and Marsala

MAKES 4 TO 6 SERVINGS

This wonderful recipe, a specialty of my mom Rose, is the perfect example of what to make on a busy weeknight. I always looked forward to having this on Wednesdays when its turn in our family menu rotation came up. To this day, I ask Mom to make it for me when I need perfect comfort food. Serve this with steamed rice to soak up the juices.

8 chicken drumsticks

8 bone-in chicken thighs

¼ cup olive oil

2 medium yellow onions, cut into thin half moon

1 cup Chicken Stock (page 37) or reduced-sodium store-bought chicken broth

½ cup dry white wine

¼ cup dry Marsala or more white wine

2 cups fresh or thawed frozen peas

½ cup chopped fresh basil

Salt and freshly ground black pepper

1. Preheat the oven to 450°F.

2. Toss the chicken drumsticks and thighs with the oil in a large roasting pan, and arrange them in a single layer. Roast for 15 minutes. Flip the chicken over and continue roasting for 15 minutes more.

3. Add the onions and toss with the pan juices. Roast until the onions are softened, about 5 minutes. Remove the pan from the oven. Stir in the stock, wine, and Marsala, loosening any browned bits in the pan with a wooden spoon. Stir in the peas and basil. Return to the oven and roast until the chicken thigh shows no sign of pink when pierced at the bone, and the liquid has reduced slightly, about 10 minutes more. Season to taste with salt and pepper. Transfer the chicken and pan juices to a deep platter and serve hot.

Seafood

Striped Bass Francese

Striped Bass Salad

Striped Bass with
Eggplant and Olives

Trio of Striped Bass,
Salmon, and Tilapia

Oven-Roasted Branzino with
Lemon-Mustard Vinaigrette

Fried Cod Fritters

Flounder Milanese

Pan-Seared Halibut with
Mustard-Caper Sauce

Roasted Monkfish with
Asparagus and Chickpeas

Fillet of Sole with Seafood Stuffing

Grilled Calamari with
Three Bean Salad

Octopus Affogati with Linguine

Scallops Oreganata

Sea Scallops with
Caramelized Fennel

Sautéed Shrimp with
Prosecco Sauce

Striped Bass Francese

I used to fish with my dad and cousins off Orient Point in Long Island, and we could serve the catch at the restaurant. Now, we buy seafood from certified purveyors, and that's not a bad thing. This is one of my favorite ways to serve one of my favorite fish, with a light egg coating and delicate lemon sauce.

½ cup olive oil

½ cup all-purpose flour

2 large eggs

Four 6-ounce skinless striped bass fillets

1 cup bottled clam juice or water

6 tablespoons fresh lemon juice

⅓ cup dry white wine

¼ cup chopped fresh basil

2 tablespoons cold unsalted butter

1 tablespoon chopped fresh flat-leaf parsley

Salt and freshly ground black pepper

1. Heat the oil in a large skillet over medium-high heat until the oil is shimmering but not smoking.

2. Line a large rimmed baking sheet with paper towels. Spread the flour on a plate. Beat the eggs in a shallow bowl. Coat each fillet in flour, shake off the excess, and dip on both sides in the beaten eggs. Add the fillets to the skillet and cook, turning once, until golden brown on both sides, about 2 minutes. Using a slotted spatula, transfer the fillets to the paper towel–lined baking sheet.

3. Carefully pour off the oil from the skillet. Return the skillet to medium heat. Add the clam juice, lemon juice, wine, basil, butter, and parsley. Bring to a boil, whisking almost constantly to emulsify the butter into the liquid. Return the fish to the skillet and simmer, uncovered, until the fish is opaque when pierced with the tip of a sharp knife, and the sauce has thickened, 4 to 5 minutes. Season to taste with salt and pepper. Transfer each fillet to a dinner plate and spoon the sauce on top.

Striped Bass Salad

MAKES 4 SERVINGS

Putting on an extra few pounds is an occupational hazard in the restaurant business. We designed this salad to enjoy at lunch when we want to eat something on the light side. You can use less garlic if you wish . . . but we don't. Don't marinate the fish for more than an hour or the texture will be affected.

DRESSING

1/2 cup fresh lemon juice

8 garlic cloves, minced

2/3 cup extra-virgin olive oil

2 celery ribs, cut into 1/2-inch dice

1/2 cup coarsely chopped pitted kalamata olives

1/2 cup chopped fresh basil

Salt and freshly ground black pepper

Four 6-ounce skinless striped bass fillets

1. To make the dressing: Whisk the lemon juice and garlic together in a medium bowl. Gradually whisk in the oil. Add the celery, olives, and basil, and whisk to combine. Season to taste with salt and pepper. Set aside for 30 minutes to 2 hours to blend the flavors.

2. Pour enough water into a large deep skillet to come 1 inch up the sides and bring to a boil over high heat. Add the fillets and reduce the heat to low. Cover and simmer until the fish is barely opaque when pierced in the thickest part with the tip of a knife, 8 to 10 minutes. Using a slotted spatula, carefully transfer the fillets to a large platter.

3. Whisk the sauce again and pour over the fish. Tilt the platter so the dressing collects in a pool, and baste it over the fish several times. Refrigerate the platter until the fish has cooled, at least 15 minutes or up to 1 hour. Serve cool or chilled.

"Sal makes the best meatballs in New York . . . they taste like my mother made them"
—*Frankie Valli*

Striped Bass with Eggplant and Olives

Eggplant is a big part of Southern Italian cooking, and we use it in a lot of recipes. Striped bass has a meaty quality and firm texture that allows it to stand up to the eggplant and other bold flavors here.

2 small globe eggplants (about 1 pound each), peeled and cut into ¹/₂-inch pieces

8 tablespoons olive oil

1 medium yellow onion, chopped

2 large beefsteak tomatoes, cut into ¹/₄-inch dice

¹/₂ cup sliced pitted kalamata olives

¹/₃ cup chopped fresh basil

¹/₂ cup water, plus more as needed

Four 6-ounce skinless striped bass fillets

¹/₄ cup dry white wine

Salt and freshly ground black pepper

1. Preheat the oven to 450°F. Toss the eggplant with 6 tablespoons of the oil on a large rimmed baking sheet. Spread the eggplant in a single layer. Roast, stirring occasionally, until the eggplant is tender, about 20 minutes.

2. Meanwhile, heat the remaining 2 tablespoons oil in a large deep skillet over medium heat. Add the onion and cook, stirring occasionally, until translucent, about 3 minutes. Add the tomatoes, olives, basil, and water and bring to a boil. Season to taste with salt and pepper. Reduce the heat to medium-low and cover. Cook at a steady simmer until the tomatoes have given off their juices, about 4 minutes.

3. Add the fillets and pour the wine over them. Cover the skillet and simmer, adding a few tablespoons of water if the tomato sauce gets too thick, until the fish is barely opaque when flaked with the tip of a knife in its thickest part, about 8 minutes. During the last 2 minutes, scatter the eggplant over the fish and cover to reheat it.

4. Transfer each fillet to a plate and spoon the eggplant mixture next to each one. Serve hot.

Trio of Striped Bass, Salmon, and Tilapia

Sometimes a customer can't decide between the different fish dishes on the menu, so we offer them this trio of bass with tomato sauce, salmon with mustard sauce, and tilapia with pesto. Because the sauces are made ahead, and the fish can be cooked together, it really isn't a difficult dish to pull off. And it just happens to feature the colors of the Italian flag.

PESTO

2 cups packed cups fresh basil leaves

$^1/_2$ cup freshly grated Parmigiano-Reggiano cheese

2 tablespoons pine nuts

3 garlic cloves, coarsely chopped

$^2/_3$ cup extra-virgin olive oil, plus more for storage

Salt

1 pound each skinless striped bass, salmon, and tilapia fillets, cut into 4 equal portions

3 tablespoons cold unsalted butter, cut into small cubes

6 tablespoons fresh lemon juice

Sweet paprika, for sprinkling

1 cup Tomato Sauce (page 100), heated

1 cup Mustard Sauce (page 88)

1. To make the pesto: Pulse the basil, cheese, pine nuts, and garlic in a food processor until the basil is finely chopped. With the machine running, gradually add the oil through the feed tube. Season to taste with salt. Transfer to a bowl. Pour a thin film of oil over the surface of the pesto to prevent discoloring and cover tightly. Whisk well before using.

2. Preheat the oven to 450°F.

3. Arrange the striped bass, salmon, and tilapia in a single layer (or overlapping slightly) in a large flame proof baking dish and dot with the butter. Pour the lemon juice and $^1/_3$ cup water over and around the fish and sprinkle with the paprika.

4. Bake until the fish looks opaque when flaked in the thickest part with the tip of a knife, 18 to 20 minutes. Remove the baking dish with the fish from the oven.

5. Position the broiler rack about 6 inches from the heat source and preheat the broiler on high.

6. Top each striped bass fillet with about ¼ cup of the tomato sauce. Top each salmon fillet with ¼ cup of the mustard sauce. Top each tilapia fillet with ¼ cup of the pesto. Broil until the sauces are hot and tinged golden brown, 1 to 2 minutes. Using a metal spatula, transfer one piece each of the striped bass, salmon, and tilapia fillet per serving to a dinner plate. Serve hot.

Oven-Roasted Branzino with Lemon-Mustard Vinaigrette

MAKES 2 SERVINGS

Branzino (which is really the Northern Italian name for European sea bass) is a mild, flaky fish that is especially tasty when it is roasted at high heat. I've never seen branzino filleted, and it seems to always be cooked on the bone. You only get two smallish fillets from each fish, so plan to have a couple of side dishes to go alongside. If you are nervous about deboning the fish at the table, even though I've given detailed instructions, go ahead and do it in the privacy of the kitchen.

SAUCE

3 tablespoons fresh lemon juice

1 teaspoon Dijon mustard

1 garlic clove, minced

¾ cup extra-virgin olive oil

Salt and freshly ground black pepper

2 whole branzino, about 1½ pounds each, scaled, cleaned, rinsed, and patted dry

6 tablespoons fresh lemon juice

¼ cup olive oil

5 garlic cloves, thinly sliced

1 tablespoon chopped fresh flat-leaf parsley

1. Preheat the oven to 450°F. Lightly oil a large flameproof baking dish.

2. To make the sauce: Whisk the lemon juice, mustard, and garlic together in a small bowl. Gradually whisk in the oil. Season to taste with salt and pepper.

3. Arrange the fishes side by side in the baking dish. Whisk ½ cup water with the lemon juice, oil, garlic, and parsley. Season to taste with salt and pepper. Pour the lemon mixture over the fish. Cover the baking dish with aluminum foil.

4. Bake until the fish is opaque when flaked with the tip of a knife in the thickest part, 35 to 40 minutes. Remove the baking dish with the fish from the oven.

5. Position the broiler rack about 6 inches from the heat source and preheat the broiler on high. Broil the fish until the fish skin blisters and begins to brown, about 2 minutes.

6. Using a large, wide spatula, carefully transfer one fish to a carving board. Using a knife, cut off the head and tail. Slide the tip of a soup spoon underneath the skin to loosen it. Using the spoon and a fork, lift

Salt and freshly ground black pepper

off and discard the skin. Now run the spoon along the spine bone to loosen the flesh. Use the spoon and fork to lift off the top fillet from the fish frame and transfer it to a dinner plate. Lift off and discard the fish frame. Loosen the bottom fillet from the skin, and use the spoon and fork to transfer it to the plate. Moisten the fillets with a spoonful of the cooking juices. Repeat with the second fish. Serve immediately with the sauce passed on the side.

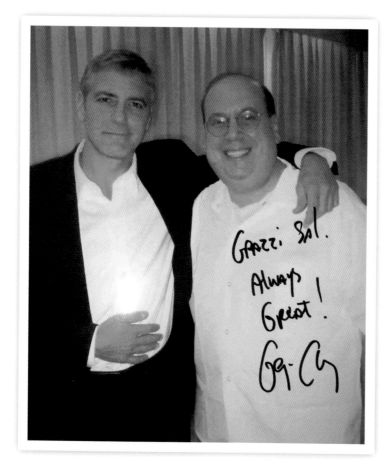

Since I have a picture of my mom eating at Patsy's when she was pregnant with me, I can honestly say that I've been going to Patsy's since BEFORE I was born. It's been a great part of my life ever since.

—George Clooney

Fried Cod Fritters

MAKES 6 SERVINGS

Just about everyone loves to indulge in golden brown fritters, hot from the oil. These are usually made from baccalà (salt cod), but a long time ago, Patsy started making his with the trimmings from fresh cod. I actually prefer them this way, and if no one is looking, I'll have mine with tartar sauce, which is not very Italian, but very good.

2¹⁄₂ pounds skinless cod fillets

BATTER

3 cups all-purpose flour

3 cups water

1 teaspoon salt

¹⁄₂ teaspoon freshly ground black pepper

¹⁄₂ teaspoon ground turmeric

¹⁄₂ teaspoon baking powder

Olive oil, for deep-frying

Lemon wedges, for serving

1. Pour enough lightly salted water into a large skillet to come halfway up the sides and bring to a boil over high heat. Add the cod and reduce the heat to medium-low. Simmer until the fish looks opaque when flaked with a fork, about 5 minutes. Drain the fish and let cool. Flake the fish into large bite-size pieces with a fork. (The cod can be covered and refrigerated for 8 hours.)

2. Line a baking sheet with paper towels. Whisk the flour, 3 cups water, salt, pepper, turmeric, and baking powder together in a large bowl.

3. Preheat the oven to 200°F. Pour enough oil to come halfway up the sides of a large deep skillet and heat the oil until it is shimmering but not smoking, or reads 350°F on a deep-frying thermometer. Working in batches, without crowding, dip the fish chunks in the batter, let the excess batter drain back into the bowl, and transfer to the hot oil. Fry, turning once, until the fritters are golden brown, 3 minutes. Using a slotted spoon, transfer them to the paper towels–lined baking sheet and keep warm in the oven while frying the remaining fritters. Serve hot with the lemon wedges.

Flounder Milanese

This is a sure-fire way to get kids to eat their fish. I know a lot of grown-ups that love fish cooked this way, too. Milanese is synonymous with crumb-coated food fried until crisp and golden. It is especially good with flounder because the coating protects the fragile flesh.

½ cup all-purpose flour

3 large eggs

1 cup Seasoned Bread Crumbs (page 14)

4 skinless flounder fillets, 6 to 8 ounces each

1 cup olive oil

Salt and freshly ground black pepper

Lemon wedges, for serving

1. Spread the flour on a plate. Beat the eggs in a shallow bowl. Spread the bread crumbs in another shallow bowl. Coat each fillet in the flour and shake off the excess. Dip in the eggs, then coat with the bread crumbs, patting the crumbs to help them adhere. Transfer to a large plate and refrigerate for 15 minutes.

2. Line a baking sheet with paper towels. Heat the oil in a large deep skillet over medium-high heat until the oil is shimmering but not smoking. Add the fillets and fry, turning once, until golden brown, about 4 minutes. Using a slotted spoon, transfer to the paper towel–lined baking sheet to drain. Season to taste with salt and pepper. Transfer the fillets to a platter and serve hot, with the lemon wedges.

"Frank Sinatra introduced me to the legendary Patsy's and I have been a fan ever since. As Sinatra used to say, 'This food is cuckoo good, Q!'"
—*Quincy Jones*

Pan-Seared Halibut with Mustard-Caper Sauce

MAKES 4 SERVINGS

Halibut is firm and meaty, and this mustard sauce works as a good counterpoint. Let the pan get good and hot before adding the fish, because you want it to have a nice caramelized crust for extra flavor.

SAUCE

2 tablespoons
fresh lemon juice

2 tablespoons
Dijon mustard

$1/3$ cup mayonnaise

2 tablespoons drained
nonpareil capers, rinsed

2 tablespoons
minced yellow onion

Freshly ground black pepper

2 tablespoons olive oil

4 skinless halibut fillets,
8 to 10 ounces each and
cut 1 inch thick

$1/3$ cup dry white wine

1. To make the sauce: Whisk the lemon juice and mustard together in a small bowl. Gradually whisk in the mayonnaise. Add the capers and onion and whisk to combine. Season to taste with the pepper. Cover and let stand for at least 15 minutes to meld the flavors.

2. Preheat the oven to 450°F.

3. Heat the olive oil in a large ovenproof skillet over high heat until the oil is very hot but not smoking. Add the halibut and cook, turning once, just until seared and golden on both sides, about 2 minutes. Transfer the halibut to a plate.

4. Reduce the heat to medium. Pour in the wine and scrape up the browned bits in the skillet with a wooden spoon. Remove from the heat and return the halibut to the skillet. Spoon the wine in the skillet over the halibut.

5. Transfer the skillet with the halibut to the oven and bake until the halibut looks opaque when pierced in the center with the tip of a knife, 8 to 10 minutes. Remove from the oven.

6. Position the broiler rack about 8 inches from the heat source and preheat the broiler. Spread the sauce over the halibut. Broil until the sauce begins to brown, 1 to 2 minutes. Transfer each fillet to a dinner plate and spoon the pan juices around the fish. Serve hot.

Roasted Monkfish with Asparagus and Chickpeas

MAKES 4 SERVINGS

Like many people, as I got older, I developed food allergies. I was pretty disappointed when I found out that I had to avoid crustaceans, but then I discovered monkfish. It has a sweet flavor and firm texture that is highly reminiscent of lobster. It's not that easy to find at a supermarket, so if it shows up, try this.

¼ cup olive oil

½ cup all-purpose flour

4 skinless monkfish fillets, about 6 ounces each

1 cup canned crushed tomatoes

One 15-ounce can chickpeas (garbanzo beans), drained and rinsed

12 asparagus spears, woody ends snapped off, stalks cut on the diagonal into 1-inch pieces

2 scallions (white and green parts), thinly sliced

Salt and freshly ground black pepper

2 tablespoons unsalted butter, cut into small cubes

1. Preheat the oven to 450°F.

2. Heat the oil in a large ovenproof skillet over medium-high. Spread the flour on a large plate. Coat the monkfish in the flour and shake off the excess. Add the monkfish to the skillet and cook, turning once, until lightly browned, about 4 minutes. Transfer to a clean plate.

3. Add the crushed tomatoes, chickpeas, asparagus, and scallions to the skillet and stir well. Bring to a boil. Season to taste with salt and pepper. Remove from the heat. Return the monkfish to the skillet and dot with the butter.

4. Transfer the skillet with the fish mixture to the oven and bake until the monkfish looks opaque when pierced in the thickest part with the tip of a knife, 18 to 20 minutes. Transfer the monkfish to a platter and spoon the sauce on top. Serve hot.

Fillet of Sole with Seafood Stuffing

MAKES 4 SERVINGS

My grandmother Concetta loved this elegant seafood dish, which is perfect for entertaining special guests at home. You can make them well ahead of time, and just bake and broil just before serving. The stuffing is moist and juicy, with a secret ingredient of ground calamari.

STUFFING

1/2 pound cleaned calamari, bodies and tentacles, cut into 1/2-inch rings

1/4 cup olive oil

1/2 cup finely chopped yellow onions

3 medium (21/25 count) shrimp, peeled and deveined, finely chopped

1/2 cup bottled clam juice

2 tablespoons dry white wine

3 tablespoons fresh lemon juice

1 tablespoon unsalted butter, at room temperature

1 tablespoon chopped fresh flat-leaf parsley

1 tablespoon seedless raisins

1 tablespoon pine nuts

1. To make the stuffing: Bring 2 quarts of water to boil in a large saucepan over high heat. Reduce the heat to medium-low to bring the water to a simmer. Add the calamari squid and cook, uncovered, until the squid is tender, 20 to 25 minutes. Drain and let cool. Pulse the calamari in a food processor until finely chopped (or chop the calamari with a large knife).

2. Heat the oil in a large skillet over medium heat. Add the onions and cook, stirring occasionally, until translucent, about 3 minutes. Stir in the chopped calamari, shrimp, clam juice, wine, lemon juice, butter, parsley, raisins, and pine nuts and bring to a boil. Reduce the heat to medium-low and stir in the cream. Simmer until the cream reduces slightly, about 2 minutes. Remove from heat. Gradually stir in the bread crumbs to make a thick paste. Let cool.

3. Preheat the oven to 450°F. Lightly butter a 10 by 15-inch glass or ceramic flame proof baking dish with softened butter. Cut each fish fillet in half, following the central line that runs the length of the fillet. Crisscross two fillets to resemble a cross. Spoon about 3 tablespoons of the stuffing at intersection of the fillet strips. Fold the ends of the horizontal fillet over and onto the stuffing. Fold the ends of the vertical fillet over to enclose the filling. Place the packet, smooth side up, in the baking dish. Repeat with the remaining fillets and stuffing. (The fish packets can be covered and refrigerated for up to 3 hours.) Pour the lemon juice over the fish packets and dot with the butter.

¼ cup light cream or
half-and-half

½ cup plain
dried bread crumbs

4 skinless sole fillets, about
8 ounces each

3 tablespoons
fresh lemon juice

2 tablespoons unsalted butter, cut into small cubes

Sweet paprika, for sprinkling

Lemon wedges, for serving

4. Bake until the fish looks opaque when flaked in the center with the tip of a knife, 16 to 18 minutes. Remove the dish with the fish packets from the oven.

5. Position the broiler rack about 6 inches from the heat source and pre-heat the broiler on high. Sprinkle the paprika over the fish packets. Broil until the tops of the packets brown lightly, about 2 minutes.

6. Transfer each fish packet to a dinner plate and top with the pan juices. Serve hot, with the lemon wedges.

Ava and Frank, Show Business Royalty

There was a time in the early fifties when Frank's career was overshadowed by that of his wife, sex goddess and movie star Ava Gardner, who was necessarily footing the bills. When Frank finally came into the chips, he was inordinately proud.

One night after his ship came in, the couple visited the restaurant. Ava was wearing a gorgeous new mink coat, which she clasped protectively around her beautiful body. Frank kept urging her to open the coat, but Patsy was nervous—for all he could tell, she could have been nude underneath the fur. Finally, she obliged, and stood up to open the coat wide. Fortunately (or unfortunately, de-pending on your outlook), she was clothed. But inside the coat was a big label reading: "THIS COAT WAS BOUGHT BY FRANK SINATRA."

Grilled Calamari with Three Bean Salad

MAKES 4 SERVINGS

Most people only fry calamari. I love it as much as the next guy, but at Patsy's, it is almost as versatile as hamburger. Dom DeLuise agreed with us. Once he came in and announced that he only wanted calamari for dinner. So he had this, a grilled calamari dish, and for dessert . . . fried calamari!

SALAD

One 15-ounce can cannellini (white kidney) beans, drained and rinsed

One 15-ounce can red kidney beans, drained and rinsed

One 15-ounce can black beans, drained and rinsed

2 scallions (green and white parts), thinly sliced

2 tablespoons balsamic vinegar

1/2 cup extra-virgin olive oil

Salt and freshly ground black pepper

MARINADE

1/2 cup extra-virgin olive oil

1. To make the salad: Combine the cannellini, red kidney, and black beans with the scallions in a medium bowl. Pour the balsamic vinegar into a small bowl and gradually whisk in the olive oil. Pour over the bean mixture, mix well, and season to taste with salt and pepper. Cover and let stand for at least 30 minutes and up to 4 hours.

2. To marinate the calamari, whisk the oil, lemon juice, basil, and garlic clove together in a shallow glass or ceramic baking dish just to combine. Season to taste with salt and pepper. Add the calamari and toss gently to combine. Cover with plastic wrap and refrigerate for 15 to 30 minutes, no longer.

3. Prepare an outdoor grill for direct cooking over medium heat (400°F). (Or preheat two grill pans over medium-high heat.)

4. Brush the grill grates clean. Drain the calamari. Place the calamari on the grill and cook, with the lid closed as much as possible, turning the calamari once, until they are seared with grill marks and have turned opaque, 4 to 5 minutes. Remove from the grill. (Or, working in batches, cook the calamari in grill pans, and keep warm on a baking sheet in a preheated 200°F oven.)

3 tablespoons
fresh lemon juice

2 tablespoons finely
chopped fresh basil

1 garlic clove, minced

Salt and freshly ground
black pepper

12 whole calamari bodies,
cleaned

Extra-virgin olive oil,
for serving

5. Spread the bean salad on a large deep platter. Arrange the calamari on top, drizzle with oil, and serve immediately.

For me, Patsy's is my home away from home. When I miss my Nonna's cooking, only one place can compare. They are wonderful people who have become like family, and I will be a fan for life.

—Michael Bublé

Octopus Affogati with Linguine

MAKES 4 SERVINGS

My dad Joe has a shellfish allergy, but he can enjoy octopus. His affection for it must be in his Neapolitan blood. Affogati means "smothered" in Italian, and here the precooked octopus is drowned in a tomato sauce. Joe says that wine corks help tenderize the very tough octopus, but that has yet to be scientifically proven. Nonetheless, I would never cook octopus any other way!

Two 1-pound octopus, heads and beaks removed

4 tablespoons extra-virgin olive oil

8 garlic cloves, finely chopped

3 cups Tomato Sauce (page 100)

¹/₄ cup chopped fresh basil

Salt and freshly ground black pepper

1 pound linguine

SPECIAL EQUIPMENT

2 to 4 natural wine corks (not synthetic corks)

1. To cook the octopus: Bring a large pot of water and the wine corks to a boil over high heat. Add the octopus, reduce the heat, and simmer at a low boil, uncovered until just tender, about 1 hour. Before draining, reserve and strain ½ cup of the cooking water. Cut the octopus into bite-size pieces and set aside.

2. Heat the olive oil in a large saucepan over medium heat and sauté the garlic for 1 to 2 minutes, or until golden. Add the octopus, tomato sauce, basil and reserved cooking water. Stir, cover, and bring to a boil. Reduce the heat and simmer, uncovered, for 20 minutes, or until sauce has thickened. Season with salt and pepper.

3. Meanwhile, bring a large pot of salted water to a boil over high heat. Add the linguine and cook according to the package directions. Drain well. Return the linguine to its cooking pot. Stir in about half of the tomato sauce and transfer to a large serving bowl.

4. Top the linguine with the remaining sauce and octopus. Serve hot.

Scallops Oreganata

MAKES 4 SERVINGS

I love to make these for my wife Lisa, who is obsessed with scallops. The crisp crumbs really sets off the sweet scallop beautifully. Use only the very best scallops here—your fish market should know if they are "dry" (see Note.) If you like a stronger oregano taste, add ½ teaspoon dried oregano to the crumbs.

2 pounds jumbo sea scallops (see Note)

½ cup bottled clam juice or water

6 tablespoons fresh lemon juice

2 tablespoons unsalted butter, cut into small cubes

Sweet paprika, for sprinkling

½ cup Seasoned Bread Crumbs (page 14)

Extra-virgin olive oil, for drizzling

2 tablespoons chopped fresh flat-leaf parsley

1. Preheat the oven to 450°F.

2. Arrange the scallops in a single layer in a large flameproof baking dish. Add the clam juice and lemon juice and dot with the butter. Sprinkle with the paprika.

3. Bake just until the scallops turn opaque but are still slightly translucent when pierced in the center with the tip of a knife, 16 to 18 minutes. Remove the baking dish with the scallops from the oven.

4. Position a broiler rack about 6 inches from the heat source and preheat on high. Sprinkle the scallops with the bread crumbs and drizzle with oil. Broil until the bread crumbs are browned, about 2 minutes. Sprinkle with the parsley and serve from the dish.

NOTE: Scallops are often soaked in sodium phosphate on the fishing boat as a preservative; this gives them an off-flavor and watery texture. "Dry" scallops, carried by the best fish markets, have not been soaked and have a much better flavor and texture. Other words to look for in choosing scallops are "diver," meaning that the scallops were harvested by hand and not trawled, or "day boat," which indicates they are collected on boats on one-day hauls to avoid the need for preservatives. These scallops are not cheap, but the "wet" scallops often taste so bad that they are a waste of money. Scallops come in sizes, like shrimp, but you usually only have a choice between large or jumbo sea scallops or small bay scallops. Ask a few questions at your fish market and to ensure that you get sweet, delicious scallops like the ones at Patsy's.

Sea Scallops with Caramelized Fennel

MAKES 4 SERVINGS

My grandparents used to serve sticks of chilled fennel to nibble between courses as a palate cleanser—a tradition that deserves to be revived. If you like fennel as much as I do, give this dish a try. The mild licorice flavor is pumped up with a dash of pastis, a French anise-based spirit. Be sure to caramelize the scallops and fennel nicely to bring out their flavors.

¼ cup plus 2 tablespoons extra-virgin olive oil

½ cup all-purpose flour

20 large sea scallops, about 1½ pounds (see Note on page 96)

1 fennel bulb, quartered, cored, and cut into ¼-inch dice

1 cup bottled clam juice or water

3 tablespoons pastis (anise-flavored liqueur), such as Pernod or Ricard

¼ cup pine nuts

¼ cup golden raisins

2 tablespoons unsalted butter

2 scallions (white and green parts), finely chopped

2 tablespoons chopped fresh flat-leaf parsley

Salt and freshly ground black pepper

1. Heat ¼ cup of the oil in a large skillet over high heat until the oil is shimmering but not smoking. Spread the flour on a plate. Working in batches, coat the scallops in the flour, shaking off the excess. Add the scallops to the skillet and cook, turning once, until golden brown on both sides but not fully cooked, about 3 minutes. Transfer to a clean plate.

2. Pour off any oil in the skillet. Add the remaining 2 tablespoons oil and heat. Stir in the fennel and reduce the heat to medium. Cook, stirring occasionally, until the fennel has softened and turned golden brown, 7 to 10 minutes.

3. Stir in the clam juice, pastis, pine nuts, raisins, and butter and bring to a boil. Return the scallops to the skillet and reduce the heat to medium-low. Cover and cook, stirring occasionally, until the sauce has thickened slightly, about 3 minutes. Sprinkle with the scallions and parsley and continue cooking, uncovered, until the scallops are barely opaque in the center when pierced with the tip of a sharp knife, about 1 minute more. Using a slotted spoon, transfer the scallops to a deep platter. Return the skillet to high heat and boil the sauce, stirring often, until it is thick enough to coat a wooden spoon, about 1 minute. Season to taste with salt and pepper. Pour the sauce over the scallops and serve hot.

Sautéed Shrimp with Prosecco Sauce

MAKES 4 SERVINGS

Often, at the end of the night, there is a bottle or two of leftover Prosecco with just enough bubbly wine left in them to make a nice sauce for shrimp before we go home. If cooking at home, it's worthwhile to open one bottle to make the sauce . . . and another to serve with the shrimp.

¼ cup olive oil

¼ cup all-purpose flour

24 extra-jumbo (16/20 count) shrimp, about 1½ pounds, peeled and deveined

6 scallions (white and green parts), thinly sliced

1 tablespoon unsalted butter

1 cup Chicken Stock (page 37) or reduced-sodium store-bought chicken broth

⅔ cup Prosecco, champagne, or any dry sparkling wine

¼ cup chopped fresh flat-leaf parsley

Salt and freshly ground black pepper

1. Heat the oil in a large skillet over medium heat until very hot but not smoking. Spread the flour on a plate. Coat the shrimp with the flour, shaking off the excess. Add the shrimp to the skillet and cook, turning once, until they turn opaque on the outside and are only partially cooked, 2 to 3 minutes. Transfer the shrimp to a clean plate.

2. Pour off any oil in the skillet. Add the scallions and butter to the skillet and cook over medium heat, stirring occasionally, until the scallions have softened, 2 to 3 minutes.

3. Stir in the stock, Prosecco, and parsley and bring to a boil. Return the shrimp to the skillet and reduce the heat to medium-low. Cover and simmer until the shrimp are opaque at the center when pierced with the tip of a knife, 3 to 4 minutes. Using a slotted spoon, transfer the shrimp to a deep serving platter.

4. Increase the heat to high and boil the sauce until it is thick enough to coat a wooden spoon, about 2 minutes. Season to taste with salt and pepper. Pour over the shrimp and serve immediately.

Pasta and Risotto

Our Tomato Sauce

Basic Egg Pasta

Fettuccine with Arugula Pesto

Linguine with Bacon and Prosciutto

Rigatoni with Broccoli Rabe and Sausage

Giovanna's Penne with Cauliflower and Anchovy Tomato Sauce

Cheese Manicotti

Frittata with Linguine and Meat Sauce

Fettuccine with Parmigiano, Butter, and Sage Sauce

Fusilli with Garlic and Anchovies

Linguine with Lobster Sauce

Spaghetti and Veal Meatballs

Whole Wheat Spaghetti Provençal with Olives and Garlic

Linguine Puttanesca

Rigatoni Quattro Formaggi with Sausage

Linguine with Roasted Red Pepper Pesto

Penne with Vodka Sauce

Fusilloni with Veal, Cream, and Tomato Sauce

Penne with Wild Boar Ragù

Risotto Pescatore

Our Tomato Sauce

MAKES ABOUT 7 CUPS

Patsy's is proud to call itself a "red sauce" restaurant. Our red sauce is as good as it gets: it's based on the one that my grandmother Concetta used to make in a huge pot on her stove in Forest Hills, Queens. She would often use fresh plum tomatoes, but it is just as good—and easier—when made with high-quality San Marzano canned tomatoes. I suggest making a double batch and freezing some to have ready when you need it. Or just buy a jar of our tomato sauce.

¼ cup olive oil

1 small yellow onion, finely chopped

3 garlic cloves, halved

Two 28–ounce cans whole San Marzano tomatoes in juice

2 tablespoons hearty red wine

2 bay leaves

2 tablespoons tomato paste

¼ cup chopped fresh basil

1 tablespoon chopped fresh flat–leaf parsley

Salt and freshly ground black pepper

1. Heat the oil in a large saucepan over medium heat. Add the onion and garlic and cook, stirring occasionally, until golden, about 3 minutes. Meanwhile, pour the tomatoes and their juices into a large bowl and crush the tomatoes between your fingers until they are in chunks. Pour into the saucepan with the wine and bay leaves and bring to a boil.

2. Reduce the heat to medium-low and cover. Simmer, stirring occasionally, and cook for 35 minutes. Discard the bay leaves and continue simmering until the tomato juices have thickened, about 25 minutes. Stir in the tomato paste, basil, and parsley, and simmer, uncovered, for 5 minutes more. Season to taste with salt and pepper. Discard the garlic. (Now you know the secret to our sauce: It has garlic flavor, but no bits of garlic.)

Variation

Fresh Tomato Sauce: Make this when you come across beautiful plum (Roma) tomatoes at the market in the summer. Substitute 4½ pounds of ripe tomatoes for the canned tomatoes. Bring a pot of water to a boil over high heat. Using a small sharp knife, cut the stem core out of each tomato. Working in batches, add the tomatoes to the water and blanch just until the skins loosen, about 2 minutes. Using a wire strainer, transfer the tomatoes to a large bowl of cold water. Drain well. Remove the skins. Coarsely chop the tomatoes. Use as directed above.

Basic Egg Pasta

MAKES ABOUT 1 POUND, 2 OUNCES

We have our fresh pasta delivered from an establishment that has been in business even longer than we have. Fresh pasta cut into fettuccine and linguine is available at supermarkets, but the sheets needed for lasagna and manicotti are not easy to find. (That's because even pasta shops cut sheets into strands or shape them into ravioli.) Here's how to make egg pasta at home the way countless Italian cooks still do every day. Hand-cranked pasta machines can be purchased at kitchenware stores or online. The pasta roller attachment for some brands of heavy-duty stand mixers works very well and is quite fast.

3 large eggs, at room temperature

2 tablespoons water

1 tablespoon extra-virgin olive oil

2¼ cups all-purpose flour, or as needed

SPECIAL EQUIPMENT

A hand-cranked pasta machine or a pasta rolling (not extruding) attachment for a heavy-duty stand mixer.

1. To make the dough with a mixer: Combine the eggs, water, and oil together in the bowl of a heavy-duty stand mixer. Fit with the paddle attachment and mix on low speed to combine. Gradually add enough of the flour to make a soft, pliable dough that cleans the sides of the bowl. Change to the dough hook. Knead with the mixer on medium-low speed, adding more flour if the dough sticks to the bowl, until the dough is smooth and supple, about 5 minutes.

To make the dough by hand: Put 2 cups flour in a large bowl and make a well in the center. Add the eggs, water, and oil to the well. Using a fork, beat the egg mixture to combine, being sure not to mix in any of the flour at this point. Stir the egg mixture with the fork, then gradually begin drawing in the flour, until all of the flour has been combined with the egg mixture to make a moist, shaggy dough. Knead the dough in the bowl a few times to smooth it out. Turn out the dough onto a floured work surface. Knead, adding more flour as necessary, until the dough is smooth and supple, about 8 minutes.

2. Shape the dough into a ball, wrap in plastic wrap, and let stand at room temperature for 30 minutes to 1 hour.

3. Set up the pasta machine according to the manufacturer's instructions. Divide the dough into sixths. Working with one-sixth at a time, keeping the other portions covered with plastic wrap, shape the dough into a thick rectangle about 3 by 4-inches. Dust the dough with flour on both sides. With the machine on its widest setting, pass the short end of the dough through the rollers a few times, folding the dough in half lengthwise after each pass, and dusting with flour as needed to keep it from sticking. When the dough begins to smooth out, move the dial to the next setting. Repeat, flouring and folding the dough for two to three more passes, and passing the dough through progressively narrower rollers until the pasta is a long sheet about $\frac{1}{16}$ inch thick. Drape the sheet over the back of a straight-backed chair, which allows the pasta to air-dry on both sides. You may need to use two chairs. (You could hang the strips on a pasta drying rack, but really, the chairs work fine. Or cover a table with a tablecloth, lightly dust the cloth with flour, and lay the pasta strips on the table, turning them often as they dry to avoid sticking.)

4. Let the pasta dry, turning it occasionally to discourage sticking to the chair top, until it has a somewhat leathery, but not brittle, texture, 30 minutes to 1 hour, depending on the ambient temperature and humidity. For lasagna and manicotti, use a large knife to cut the dough into the desired size. For fettuccine, cut the dough into 12-inch lengths, then dust with flour and pass through the fettuccine cutters on the pasta machine. (Or fit the mixer with the fettuccine cutter attachment.) Place the pasta on a rimmed baking sheet, toss with flour, and let stand at room temperature until ready to cook, up to 8 hours.

Patsy's on West Fifty-sixth Street is one of my all-time favorite restaurants. I have wonderful memories of going there with my dad and Uncle Frank as a teenager in the 1950s. It feels like home, but with better food! Fortunately, Sal and his people have continued the tradition generation after generation. The magic in Patsy's kitchen has been going on for decades and the result is that many of the families of his devoted patrons have also become lifetime fans. —Deana Martin

Fettuccine with Arugula Pesto

Arugula has a peppery, strong flavor, and while I love it in salad, I've discovered that it also makes an excellent pesto with the arugula standing in for basil. Crunchy and buttery toasted pine nuts give the pasta a nice finishing touch.

ARUGULA PESTO

1/2 cup pine nuts

1 large garlic clove, peeled

One 5-ounce bag baby arugula

1/4 cup freshly grated Parmigiano-Reggiano cheese

1/3 cup extra-virgin olive oil

Salt and freshly ground black pepper

1 1/4 pounds fresh fettuccine

1/4 cup light cream or half-and-half

1/4 cup freshly grated Parmigiano-Reggiano cheese, plus more for serving

1. To make the pesto: Heat a medium skillet over medium heat. Add the pine nuts and cook, stirring often, until golden brown, 2 to 3 minutes. Transfer to a plate and let cool.

2. With the machine running, drop the garlic clove through the feed tube of a food processor and process until minced. Add 2 tablespoons of the pine nuts along with the arugula and the grated cheese. Process until the arugula is minced. With the machine running, gradually pour the oil through the feed tube to make a thick pesto. Season to taste with salt and pepper. Transfer to a bowl and press plastic wrap directly on the surface of the pesto. (The pesto can be stored at room temperature for up to 4 hours.)

3. Bring a large pot of salted water to a boil over high heat. Add the fettuccine and cook according to the package directions until al dente. Scoop out and reserve 1/2 cup of the cooking water. Drain the pasta well. Return the fettuccine to its cooking pot.

4. Add the pesto, light cream, the 1/4 cup grated cheese, and the reserved cooking water to the fettuccine and bring to a simmer over low heat, stirring constantly. Transfer to a large serving bowl and sprinkle with the remaining 6 tablespoons toasted pine nuts. Serve hot, with more Parmigiano cheese passed on the side.

Linguine with Bacon and Prosciutto

MAKES 4 SERVINGS

This is my take on pasta carbonara, one of the richest pastas on the planet. The eggs and Parmigiano-Reggiano give the sauce a creamy quality that is hard to resist. And I love the combination of bacon and prosciutto—if one pork product is good, then two are better, right?

---

6 slices bacon, cut into ½-inch pieces

Half a ⅛-inch-thick slice prosciutto, cut into ⅛-inch-wide strips

⅓ cup extra-virgin olive oil

2 medium onions, finely chopped

1 pound linguine

½ cup freshly grated Parmigiano-Reggiano cheese, plus more for serving

3 large eggs, beaten

Salt and freshly ground black pepper

¼ cup fresh basil chiffonade (see page 8)

1. Bring a large pot of salted water to a boil over high heat.

2. Meanwhile, cook the bacon in medium skillet over medium heat, stirring often, until crisp and browned, about 6 minutes. During the last minute or so, stir in the prosciutto. Using a slotted spoon, transfer the bacon and prosciutto to paper towels to drain.

3. Pour out the fat and wipe out the skillet. Add the oil to the skillet and heat over medium heat. Add the onions and cook, stirring occasionally, until lightly browned, about 4 minutes. Set the onions aside.

4. Add the linguine to the boiling water and cook according to the package directions until al dente. Scoop out and reserve 1 cup of the pasta cooking water. Drain the linguine.

5. Add the reserved onions, reserved pasta water, bacon, and the prosciutto to the pasta cooking pot and bring to a boil. Add the drained linguine and grated cheese and mix well. Reduce the heat to very low. Stirring constantly, mix in the beaten eggs and cook just until the sauce thickens, about 30 seconds; do not boil. Remove from the heat and season to taste with salt and pepper.

6. Transfer to a large serving bowl and top with the basil. Serve hot, with more Parmigiano cheese passed on the side.

Rigatoni with Broccoli Rabe and Sausage

MAKES 4 TO 6 SERVINGS

Hearty with sausage and broccoli rabe, this is a filling pasta that can be served as a main course meal. Patsy's version has a little bacon in it, too, as well as provolone to smooth out the bitterness of the broccoli rabe.

1 pound broccoli rabe, ends trimmed, very coarsely chopped

1/4 cup plus 1 tablespoon extra-virgin olive oil

1 medium yellow onion, diced

2 garlic cloves, minced

2 cups water

12 ounces hot Italian pork sausages, casings removed, cut into bite-size pieces

2 slices bacon, cut into 1/2-inch pieces

1 cup coarsely chopped canned Italian plum tomatoes

Salt and freshly ground black pepper

3/4 cup shredded mild provolone cheese (3 ounces)

1 pound rigatoni

1/2 cup ricotta cheese, at room temperature, for serving

1. Wash the broccoli rabe well in a large bowl of cold water. Lift the broccoli rabe out of the bowl and transfer to another bowl, leaving any grit behind in the first bowl. Do not dry the broccoli rabe.

2. Heat 1/4 cup of the oil in a large saucepan over medium heat. Add the onion and cook, stirring occasionally, until lightly browned, about 4 minutes. Stir in the garlic and cook until fragrant, about 1 minute. Add the wet broccoli rabe with the 2 cups water and bring to a boil. Cover and reduce the heat to medium-low. Cook, stirring occasionally, until the broccoli rabe is tender, 10 to 12 minutes. Remove from the heat and cover tightly to keep warm.

3. Heat the remaining 1 tablespoon oil in a large skillet over medium heat. Add the sausage and cook, crumbling the sausage as it cooks with the side of a spoon until browned, about 8 minutes. Using a slotted spoon, transfer the sausage to the broccoli rabe.

4. Pour out any fat from the skillet. Add the bacon to the skillet and cook, stirring often, until crisp and browned, about 6 minutes.

5. Meanwhile, bring a large pot of salted water to a boil over high heat.

6. Using a slotted spoon, add the bacon to the broccoli rabe mixture. Stir in the tomatoes. Return the broccoli rabe mixture to medium heat and bring to a boil. Reduce the heat to medium-low and cover. Simmer, stirring occasionally, to meld the flavors, about 5 minutes. Season to taste with salt and pepper. Reduce the heat to very low and cover to keep the sauce warm.

7. Add the rigatoni to the boiling water and cook according to the package directions until al dente. Drain well and return the rigatoni to its cooking pot. Add the provolone cheese and about one-quarter of the broccoli rabe sauce and mix well to melt the cheese. Transfer to a large serving bowl and top with the remaining sauce. Spoon into individual bowls, and top each serving with a dollop of the ricotta.

Time Spares No One

I have only seen my dad cry three times: At his dad's funeral, at his mother's funeral, and after a visit from Sinatra. It was in Frank's later years, when time was catching up with him, and his memory was becoming very unreliable. We were all sitting upstairs when Frank looked sad and said, "I really miss that guy." Dad asked, "Who do you mean, Frank?" The Chairman answered, "You know, the little guy with one eye. What was his name?" My dad was so choked up that he had to leave the table. Frank could not remember the name of Sammy Davis, Jr., with whom he had entertained millions.

Giovanna's Penne with Cauliflower and Anchovy Tomato Sauce

MAKES 4 TO 6 SERVINGS

My wife's grandmother, Giovanna, came from Sicily. She cooked a full meal every day for as long as she was able. She taught us all how to make a great meal with humble ingredients.

1 cup Seasoned Bread Crumbs (page 14)

¼ cup olive oil

4 garlic cloves, minced

One 2-ounce can anchovies in oil, drained and chopped

One 28-ounce can crushed tomatoes

1 small head cauliflower, broken into florets

¼ cup chopped fresh basil

1 pound penne

1. Position the broiler rack about 6 inches from the heat source. Spread the bread crumbs on a small rimmed baking sheet. Broil, stirring occasionally, until the bread crumbs are toasted, 1 to 2 minutes. Let cool.

2. Place a steamer insert in a large saucepan. Add enough cold water to come just short of the insert and bring to a boil over medium heat. Add the cauliflower and cover tightly. Steam until the cauliflower is crisp-tender, about 5 minutes. Remove from the heat and uncover.

3. Heat the oil and garlic together in a large saucepan over medium heat, stirring often, until the garlic softens, about 2 minutes. Add the anchovies and cook, mashing them into the oil, about 1 minute. Stir in the tomatoes and bring to a boil. Reduce the heat to medium-low. Simmer, stirring occasionally, until slightly thickened, about 35 minutes. Add the cauliflower and basil and cook until the cauliflower is very tender, 10 to 15 minutes.

4. Meanwhile, bring a large pot of salted water to a boil over high heat. Add the penne and cook according to the package directions until al dente. Drain the penne and return it to its cooking pot. Add the sauce and stir well. Transfer to a large serving bowl and top with the half of the bread crumbs. Serve hot, and pass the remaining bread crumbs.

Cheese Manicotti

You can buy dried manicotti shells at the supermarket, but if you are a Scognamillo, you only make your "mani-got" with fresh pasta. (If you are making this with homemade pasta, you may have to piece together a couple of sheets to get the right size.) This is yet another Patsy's recipe everyone expects to contain a secret ingredient. Sorry, but it is only good ingredients and a little time.

5 cups Parmigiano–Reggiano cheese (1¼ pounds)

1½ pounds whole–milk ricotta cheese

2 pounds fresh mozzarella cheese, finely diced

2 large eggs, beaten

About 1 pound Basic Egg Pasta (page 101), cut into twelve 1-by-5-inch pasta sheets, or use store–bought.

Olive oil, for the baking dish

4 cups Tomato Sauce (page 100)

1. Mix 4¾ cups of the Parmigiano-Reggiano with the ricotta, mozzarella, and eggs in a heavy-duty stand mixer fitted with the paddle attachment on low speed until well combined. Cover and refrigerate until ready to use.

2. Bring a large pot of salted water to a boil over high heat. Add the pasta and cook (the water does not have to return to a boil) according to the directions until barely tender. (If using the Basic Egg Pasta on page 101, just cook until barely tender, about 1 minute.) Do not overcook. Drain and transfer to a large bowl of cold water.

3. Preheat the oven to 450°F. Lightly oil a 10 by 15-inch flameproof baking dish. Spread ½ cup of the tomato sauce in the baking dish. Place a clean kitchen towel in front of you on the work surface. One at a time, lift a pasta rectangle from the water and place it, short side facing you, on the towel to drain briefly. Place about ½ cup of the cheese mixture on the lower third of the pasta and roll it up into a thick cylinder. Place it, seam side down, in the baking dish. Repeat with the remaining pasta sheets and cheese mixture. Top with the remaining sauce and drizzle about ¼ cup of water around the inside edges of the dish.

4. Bake until the sauce is bubbling, about 20 minutes. Remove from the oven and sprinkle with the remaining ¼ cup Parmigiano.

5. Position the broiler rack about 8 inches from the heat source and preheat the broiler on high. Broil the manicotti until the Parmigiano is lightly browned, about 2 minutes. Let stand for 10 minutes. Serve hot.

Frittata with Linguine and Meat Sauce

MAKES 4 SERVINGS

Americans usually make frittata for breakfast or brunch with vegetables and maybe some sausage or ham. But, in Italy, it is a great way to use up leftover pasta for lunch or supper. Here's a recipe for starting from scratch, assuming you don't have leftover pasta. But you can substitute just about 4 cups of any tomato-sauce-based pasta dish for the linguine mixture.

8 ounces linguine

1 tablespoon unsalted butter

4 tablespoons olive oil

1 medium onion, peeled and diced

1/2 pound ground veal

2 cups Tomato Sauce (page 100)

3 large eggs, beaten

1/3 cup freshly grated Parmigiano-Reggiano cheese plus more for serving

Salt and freshly ground pepper

1 tablespoon chopped fresh flat-leaf parsley

1. Preheat the oven to 350°F. Meanwhile, bring a large pot of salted water to a boil over high heat. Add the linguine and cook until al dente. Drain well. Transfer the linguine to a large bowl and toss with the butter.

2. Meanwhile heat 2 tablespoons of the oil in a medium skillet over medium heat. Add the onion and cook, stirring occasionally, until lightly browned, about 4 minutes. Add the veal and cook, breaking up the veal with the side of a spoon, until it shows no sign of pink, about 5 minutes. Add the veal mixture to the linguine and mix thoroughly. Add the tomato sauce, eggs, 1/3 cup cheese, and mix gently. Remove from the heat.

3. Add 1 tablespoon of the oil to a nonstick 10-inch skillet over medium heat and heat until hot but not smoking. Add the linguine mixture and spread evenly until the underside is golden brown, about 3 minutes. Place a flat pot lid or plate on top of the skillet, hold tight, and invert so the frittata is on the lid. Set the frittata aside. Add the remaining 1 tablespoon oil to the skillet and heat. Slide the frittata from the lid into the skillet and cook until the other side is golden brown, about 3 minutes more.

4. Transfer the skillet with the frittata to the oven and bake until the frittata is puffed, about 10 minutes. Let stand for 5 minutes. Slide the frittata onto a serving plate. Season to taste with salt and pepper, and sprinkle with Parmigiano and parsley. Serve warm or at room temperature.

Fettuccine with Parmigiano, Butter, and Sage

MAKES 4 TO 6 SERVINGS

You may have noticed that we love red sauce. But here is a fantastic pasta dish that can be made in just a few minutes, with not a tomato in sight. We serve it often to customers who want a vegetarian meal. The key here is fresh sage, and lots of it.

1¼ pounds fresh fettuccine

5 tablespoons
(½ stick plus 1 tablespoon)
unsalted butter

½ cup finely chopped
fresh sage leaves

½ cup whole-milk
ricotta cheese

1 cup freshly grated
Parmigiano-Reggiano
cheese (about 4 ounces),
plus more for serving

2 tablespoons chopped
fresh flat-leaf parsley

Salt and freshly ground
black pepper

1. Bring a large pot of salted water to a boil over high heat. Add the fettuccine and cook according to the package directions until al dente. Scoop out and reserve 3½ cups of the cooking water. Drain the fettuccine. Toss with 1 tablespoon of the butter and cover to keep warm.

2. Add the remaining 4 tablespoons butter to the cooking pot and melt over medium heat. Stir in the sage and cook until fragrant, about 30 seconds. Add 3 cups of the reserved cooking water and bring to a boil over high heat. Return the heat to medium and simmer until the butter and cooking water are emulsified, about 1 minute.

3. Add the fettuccine to the sage mixture. Add the ricotta and ½ cup of Parmigiano-Reggiano and reduce the heat to very low. Mix gently until the cheeses have melted. Season to taste with salt and pepper. Transfer to a large serving bowl and sprinkle with the parsley and remaining Parmigiano. Serve hot, with more Parmigiano passed on the side.

Fusilli with Garlic and Anchovies

MAKES 4 TO 6 SERVINGS

In Naples, where there isn't a lot of grazing land and therefore, not a lot of cheese, toasted bread crumbs are often used as a pasta topping instead of Parmigiano-Reggiano or Pecorino Romano. Just ask my Sicilian mother-in-law, some of whose best dishes are made this way. On paper, this pasta doesn't look like much, but each one of its few ingredients has an important role to play.

1 cup Seasoned Bread Crumbs (page 14)

1 pound fusilli

1/3 cup plus 1 tablespoon extra-virgin olive oil

8 garlic cloves, thinly sliced

8 anchovy fillets in oil, drained and finely chopped

1/4 cup fresh basil chiffonade (see page 8)

Salt and freshly ground black pepper

1. Bring a large pot of salted water to a boil over high heat.

2. Position a broiler rack about 6 inches from the heat source and preheat the broiler on high. Spread the bread crumbs on a baking sheet. Broil, stirring occasionally, until the crumbs are lightly toasted, 2 to 3 minutes. Set the bread crumbs aside.

3. Add the fusilli to the boiling water and cook according to the package directions until al dente. Scoop out and reserve 1½ cups of the pasta cooking water. Drain the fusilli and return it to its cooking pot. Toss the fusilli with 1 tablespoon oil and cover to keep warm.

4. Meanwhile, heat the remaining ¼ cup oil and the garlic in a large deep skillet over medium heat, stirring often, until the garlic has softened, about 1 minute. Add the anchovies and mash into the oil until they dissolve and the garlic turns golden, about 1 minute more. Stir in the reserved pasta water and the basil and bring to a boil over high heat. Reduce the heat to medium and simmer briskly to meld the flavors, 1 to 2 minutes.

5. Add the anchovy sauce to the pasta and mix well. Divide the pasta among four pasta bowls and sprinkle each generously with the toasted bread crumbs. Serve immediately.

Linguine with Lobster Sauce

MAKES 4 SERVINGS

This is a good way to stretch a lobster to serve four people. If you don't want to dispatch the lobster at home, buy a cooked one and use the shells to make the sauce. My mother eats this whenever she gets the chance.

One 1½–pound lobster

¼ cup plus 1 tablespoon olive oil

4 cups Tomato Sauce (page 100)

¼ cup dry white wine

2 tablespoons chopped fresh flat–leaf parsley

½ teaspoon hot red pepper flakes

Salt

1 pound linguine, cooked until al dente, drained

1. Bring a large pot of salted water to a boil over high heat. Freeze the lobster for about 30 minutes to lull it.

2. Add the lobster to the boiling water and cover. Cook just until the lobster shell turns red, 10 to 12 minutes. Drain and rinse under cold running water until cool enough to handle.

3. On a carving board, using a sharp knife, chop the lobster at the seam behind its head into two pieces. With the back side down, cut the lobster tail in half lengthwise. Discard the dark vein from the tail. Cut off the claws and knuckles and crack them with a nutcracker. Remove the lobster meat from the tail, claws, and knuckles and cut into bite-size pieces, saving the shells from the tail and claws. Cut the lobster head in half lengthwise. If the lobster has red coral or green tomalley, reserve it with the lobster meat. Cover and refrigerate the lobster meat, coral, and tomalley.

4. Heat the oil in a large saucepan over medium heat. Add the tomato sauce, wine, and red pepper flakes, bring to a boil, and reduce the heat to medium-low. Add the reserved lobster shells and halved head. Simmer, stirring occasionally, until the sauce has slightly reduced, about 35 minutes.

5. Using tongs, remove and discard the shells and head halves. Stir in the reserved lobster meat, with the red coral and green tomalley, if using, and cook just until heated through, about 2 minutes. Season to taste with salt and pepper. Add to the linguine and stir well. Transfer to a large serving bowl and serve hot.

Spaghetti and Veal Meatballs

MAKES 4 TO 6 SERVINGS

With no false modesty, I have often heard that Patsy's has the best meatballs in New York. These tasty icons of Italian-American cuisine do have a secret ingredient: ground veal, which has more natural gelatin than ground beef or pork, and provides extra moisture. For a little while, my dad Joe took them off the menu, believing that they were old hat. I argued that the customers demanded them. As an experiment, we put them back on the menu for two days to see how many orders we sold. Our meatballs will never leave the menu again.

VEAL MEATBALLS

1½ pounds ground veal

⅓ cup plain
dried bread crumbs

2 large eggs, beaten

2 tablespoons freshly grated
Pecorino Romano cheese

1 tablespoon chopped fresh
flat-leaf parsley

1 garlic clove, minced

1 teaspoon salt

½ teaspoon freshly ground
black pepper

Pinch of dried oregano

2 cups olive oil, for frying

1 pound spaghetti

4 cups Tomato Sauce
(page 100)

Freshly grated
Parmigiano-Reggiano
cheese, for serving

1. To make the meatballs: Combine the veal, bread crumbs, eggs, Pecorino Romano, parsley, garlic, salt, pepper, and oregano in a large bowl. Using your hands, mix them together thoroughly. Roll into 12 meatballs and transfer to a plate.

2. Line a platter or baking sheet with paper towels and place near the stove. Heat the oil in a large deep skillet and heat over high heat until the oil is shimmering (350°F on a deep-frying thermometer). Working in batches, without crowding, carefully add the meatballs and fry, turning occasionally, until they are nicely browned, 4 to 5 minutes. Using a slotted spoon, transfer to the paper towels. Reheat the oil to shimmering before adding each batch.

3. Meanwhile, bring a large pot of salted water to a boil over high heat.

4. Bring the tomato sauce to a simmer in a large saucepan over medium heat. Add the meatballs and reduce the heat to medium-low. Cover the saucepan and simmer until the meatballs are cooked through, 8 to 10 minutes.

5. When the meatballs are added to the sauce, add the pasta to the boiling water and cook according to the package directions until al dente. Drain the spaghetti and return it to its cooking pot. Add about half of the tomato sauce and mix well. Divide the pasta and meatballs among pasta bowls and top with the remaining sauce. Serve hot with the Parmigiano-Reggiano passed on the side.

Whole Wheat Spaghetti Provençal with Olives and Garlic

MAKES 4 TO 6 SERVINGS

There's nothing shy about this pasta. It's very similar to a puttanesca without the tomatoes. I make it when I don't have a lot of time but want something filling. The whole wheat spaghetti brings its own robust flavor to the proceedings.

⅓ cup extra-virgin olive oil

10 garlic cloves, halved lengthwise

¾ cup coarsely chopped pitted kalamata olives

¼ cup fresh basil chiffonade (see page 8)

2 tablespoons drained nonpareil capers, rinsed

Salt and freshly ground pepper

1 pound whole wheat spaghetti

Freshly grated Parmigiano-Reggiano cheese, for serving

1. Bring a large pot of salted water to a boil over high heat.

2. Meanwhile, heat the oil and garlic together in a large skillet over medium-low heat, stirring often, until the garlic is golden and tender, about 4 minutes. Stir in the olives, basil, and capers. Cook, stirring often, until the olives are heated through, about 2 minutes. Remove from the heat.

3. Add the spaghetti to the boiling water and cook according to the package directions until al dente. Scoop out and reserve 1 cup of the cooking water. Drain the spaghetti well and return it to its cooking pot.

4. Add the olive mixture and reserved spaghetti-cooking water. Stir over low heat, just until the spaghetti has absorbed some of the sauce, about 1 minute. Transfer to a large serving bowl. Serve hot, with Parmigiano-Reggiano passed on the side.

Linguine Puttanesca

MAKES 4 SERVINGS

It's an oft-told story that puttanesca is named for the "working girls" of Naples who had to throw together a meal quickly between customers. But the sauce was so popular because of its tantalizing aroma that it drew in the clientele! At Patsy's, we serve it with lots of anchovies.

¼ cup olive oil

2 garlic cloves, peeled and finely chopped

One 28-ounce can whole plum tomatoes in juice, undrained

½ cup coarsely chopped pitted kalamata olives

3 tablespoon drained nonpareil capers, rinsed

6 anchovy fillets in oil, drained and finely chopped

1 teaspoon dried oregano

Salt and freshly ground pepper

1 pound linguine

Freshly grated Parmigiano-Reggiano cheese, for serving

1. Bring a large pot of salted water to a boil over high heat.

2. Meanwhile, heat the oil and garlic together in a large deep skillet over medium heat, stirring often, until the garlic is golden, about 2 minutes. Pour the tomato juices into the skillet. As you add the tomatoes, crush them between your fingers. Bring to a boil. Add the olives, capers, anchovies, and oregano and reduce the heat to medium-low. Simmer, stirring occasionally, until the mixture has thickened, about 20 minutes. Remove from the heat and cover to keep warm.

3. Add the linguine to the boiling water and cook according to the package directions until al dente. Scoop out and reserve ½ cup of the cooking water. Drain the linguine well and return it to its cooking pot.

4. Add the tomato sauce and the reserved pasta water and bring just to a boil over high heat. Season to taste with salt and pepper. Transfer to a large serving bowl and serve hot, with the Parmigiano-Reggiano passed on the side.

Rigatoni Quattro Formaggi with Sausage

MAKES 4 TO 6 SERVINGS

Russ Cahill has been our official "jack-of-all-trades" for almost twenty years. He eats this rib-sticking dish so often that we call it "Russ's Pasta." This is all about the four cheeses; the red sauce recedes into the background.

12 ounces Italian sausage, casings removed

1 cup Tomato Sauce (page 100)

1½ cups whole-milk ricotta cheese

¾ cup grated Parmigiano-Reggiano cheese

¾ cup (½ inch) cubed provolone cheese

¼ cup fresh basil chiffonade (see page 8)

1 pound rigatoni

1½ cups (½-inch) cubed fresh mozzarella cheese

1. Bring a large pot of salted water to a boil over high heat.

2. Heat a large skillet over medium heat. Add the sausage and cook, breaking up the meat into bite-size pieces with the side of a spoon, until it is cooked through, about 6 minutes. Add the tomato sauce and bring to a simmer. Remove from the heat and stir in the ricotta, ½ cup of the Parmigiano-Reggiano, ½ cup of the provolone, and the basil. Cover and keep the sauce warm.

3. Meanwhile add the rigatoni to the boiling water and cook according to the package directions until al dente. Scoop out and reserve 2 cups of the cooking water. Drain well, and return the rigatoni to its cooking pot. Stir in the sauce with the reserved cooking water.

4. Position the broiler rack about 6 inches from the heat source and preheat the broiler to high.

5. Lightly oil a 9 by 13-inch flameproof baking dish. Sprinkle with the mozzarella and the remaining ¼ cup Parmigiano and ¼ cup provolone. Broil until the cheeses have melted and are beginning to brown, about 2 minutes. Serve hot.

Linguine with Roasted Red Pepper Pesto

MAKES 4 TO 6 SERVINGS

This pasta takes two of my favorite ingredients, roasted red peppers and pasta, and brings them together for a party on a plate. It's also a great choice for our guests who ask for something vegetarian.

RED PEPPER PESTO

2 garlic cloves, peeled

2 large red bell peppers, roasted (see page 53)

1/3 cup extra-virgin olive oil

1/3 cup freshly grated Parmigiano-Reggiano cheese

1/4 cup packed fresh basil leaves

1/4 cup light cream or half-and-half

Salt and freshly ground black pepper

1 pound linguine

Freshly grated Parmigiano-Reggiano cheese, for serving

1. To make the pesto: With the food processor running, drop the garlic through the feed tube and process until minced. Add the roasted bell peppers, oil, grated cheese, basil, and light cream and process until smooth. Season to taste with salt and black pepper. Cover and set aside at room temperature for up to 2 hours.

2. Bring a large pot of salted water to a boil over high heat. Add the linguine and cook according to the package directions until al dente. Scoop out and reserve 1 cup of the cooking water. Drain the linguine well and return it to its cooking pot.

3. Add about three-quarters of the red pepper pesto and mix well. Mix in enough of the cooking water to make the sauce creamy. Transfer the linguine to a large serving bowl and top with the remaining pesto. Serve hot, with the grated Parmigiano-Reggiano passed on the side.

Penne with Vodka Sauce

MAKES 4 TO 6 SERVINGS

When we first started serving this pasta sauce, it was called velutto, "velvet" in Italian. That's an accurate description of this creamy tomato sauce that has become a staple in Italian restaurants around the world. No one is quite sure who first discovered how the alcohol in vodka reacts with the other ingredients to intensify their flavors. My son Joseph would eat this every day, if we let him. Don't worry! The alcohol burns off during cooking.

VODKA SAUCE

3 tablespoons olive oil

¼ cup minced yellow onion

One 28–ounce can crushed tomatoes

⅓ cup plus 1 tablespoon heavy cream

2 tablespoons vodka

1 tablespoon unsalted butter

1 tablespoon tomato paste

2 tablespoons chopped fresh basil

2 teaspoons finely chopped fresh flat–leaf parsley

¼ teaspoon hot red pepper flakes

Salt and freshly ground pepper

1 pound penne or other tube–shaped pasta

Freshly grated Parmigiano–Reggiano cheese, for serving

1. To make the sauce: Heat the olive oil in a large saucepan over medium heat. Add the onion and cook, stirring often, until translucent, about 3 minutes.

2. Stir in the crushed tomatoes and bring to a boil over high heat. Reduce the heat to medium-low and simmer, covered, stirring occasionally, until the sauce has thickened slightly, about 35 minutes. During the last 5 minutes, whisk in the cream, vodka, butter, tomato paste, basil, parsley, and red pepper flakes. Season to taste with salt and black pepper.

3. Bring a large pot of salted water to a boil over high heat. Add the penne and cook according to package directions until al dente. Drain well. Return the penne to its cooking pot. Add about three-quarters of the sauce and mix well. Transfer to a large serving bowl and top with the remaining sauce. Serve hot with the Parmigiano-Reggiano passed on the side.

Fusilloni with Veal, Cream, and Tomato Sauce

MAKES 4 TO 6 SERVINGS

We call this "lasagna in a bowl" because it has the same flavors and ingredients as lasagna but without the layering. Fusilloni itself has a nickname, too: "Fusilli on steroids." They are big curly pasta shapes that are perfect for substantial sauces like this one.

¼ cup extra-virgin olive oil

1 small yellow onion, chopped

1 pound ground veal

4 cups Tomato Sauce (page 100)

4 dried bay leaves

¼ cup fresh basil chiffonade (see page 8)

Salt and freshly ground black pepper

1 pound fusilloni or radiatore

1½ cups whole-milk ricotta cheese

½ cup freshly grated Parmigiano-Reggiano cheese

1. Bring a large pot of salted water to a boil over high heat.

2. Heat the oil in a large skillet over medium heat. Add the onion and cook, stirring often, until golden brown, about 4 minutes. Add the veal and cook, stirring often and breaking up the veal with the side of a spoon, until the veal loses its raw pink color, about 5 minutes.

3. Stir in the tomato sauce and bay leaves and bring to a boil. Reduce the heat to medium-low and cover with the lid ajar. Simmer, stirring occasionally, to blend the flavors, about 10 minutes. Remove and discard the bay leaves. Stir in the basil and season with salt and pepper. Remove from the heat and cover to keep the sauce warm.

4. Meanwhile, add the fusilloni to the boiling water and cook according to the package directions until al dente. Scoop out and reserve ½ cup of the pasta cooking water. Drain the fusilli and return it to its cooking pot. Add half of the veal sauce, the reserved pasta water, the ricotta and Parmigiano and cook over medium heat, stirring often, until the sauce comes to a simmer.

5. Transfer to a large serving bowl and top with the remaining veal sauce. Serve hot.

Penne with Wild Boar Ragù

MAKES 4 TO 6 SERVINGS

Because wild boars (and their human hunters) abound in Tuscany, you'll find this incredible, full-flavored sauce in every trattoria in the region. Wild boar may be a relative to domesticated pork, but is has a stronger flavor. It is worth searching out.

SAUCE

1 large white onion, chopped

1 1/2 pounds wild boar shoulder, trimmed and cut into 1-inch cubes (see Note)

1/3 cup extra-virgin olive oil

One 28-ounce can plum tomatoes, drained and chopped

1 cup Chicken Stock (page 37)

1/3 cup hearty red wine

2 tablespoons u nsalted butter

1/4 cup chopped fresh basil

4 dried bay leaves

Pinch of grated nutmeg

Salt and ground pepper

1 pound penne

Freshly grated Parmigiano-Reggiano Cheese, for serving

1. Working in batches, pulse the wild boar meat in a food processor until coarsely chopped. Transfer to a bowl. (Or grind the meat in a meat grinder fitted with a large-hole plate for a coarse grind.)

2. To make the sauce: In a large saucepan, heat the oil over medium heat. Add onion and cook until lightly browned, about 5 minutes. Add the ground meat and cook, stirring occasionally, until browned, about 7 minutes. Stir in tomatoes, stock, wine, butter, basil, bay leaves, and nutmeg and bring to a boil. Reduce the heat to medium-low. Simmer, uncovered, stirring occasionally, until the sauce has thickened and the meat is tender, about 1 hour. Remove and discard the bay leaves. Season to taste with salt and pepper. (The sauce can be cooled, covered, and refrigerated for up to 2 days. Or transfer the cooled sauce to an airtight container and freeze for up to 2 months. Reheat before serving.)

3. Bring a large pot of salted water to a boil over high heat. Add the penne and cook according to the package directions until al dente. Drain well. Return the penne to its cooking pot. Add about three-quarters of the sauce and mix well. Transfer to a large serving bowl and top with the remaining sauce. Serve hot with the Parmigiano-Reggiano passed on the side.

NOTE: Wild boar can be ordered online from brokenarrowranch.com, dartagnan.com, and buyexoticmeats.com.

Risotto Pescatore

MAKES 6 SERVINGS

The Scognamillos are a pasta family because we are from southern Italy, and the rice paddies are up north near Venice. But, if you ask, we will make risotto on request. We always have seafood and tomato sauce on hand, so this is one that we make quite a bit.

24 Littleneck clams, scrubbed

24 cultivated mussels (see note page 15)

¼ cup extra-virgin olive oil

1 medium yellow onion, peeled and diced

1 pound calamari, cleaned and cut into ½-inch rings

2 cups Arborio rice

⅓ cup dry white wine

2 cups Tomato Sauce (page 100)

½ pound jumbo (21/25 count) shrimp, peeled, deveined, and cut into bite-size pieces

Salt and freshly ground black pepper

½ cup fresh basil chiffonade (see page 8)

2 tablespoons chopped fresh flat-leaf parsley

Freshly grated Parmigiano-Reggiano cheese, for serving

1. Soak the clams and mussels in a large bowl of salted ice water for about an hour. Drain well. Put the clams and mussels in a pot with 1 cup of water. Cover and bring to a boil over high heat. Cook just until the shells open, 5 to 10 minutes. Using a slotted spoon, transfer the opened shellfish to a colander, discarding the unopened ones. Reserve the cooking liquid.

2. Line a wire strainer with moistened paper towels and set over medium bowl. Strain the cooking liquid through the strainer. Measure the liquid and add enough water to measure 6 cups. Put the liquid into a medium saucepan and keep hot over low heat.

3. Heat the oil in a Dutch oven over medium heat. Add the onion and garlic and cook until tender, 4 to 5 minutes. Add the rice and cook, stirring almost constantly, until it feels heavier in the spoon, about 2 minutes. Stir in the wine. Add about ¾ cup of the warm shellfish broth and cook, adjusting the heat so the rice cooks at a steady simmer, until the rice has almost absorbed all of the liquid, about 2 minutes. Continue adding the liquid, ¾ of a cup at a time, and stirring until the liquid is absorbed and the rice is al dente, about 20 minutes. If you run out of broth before the rice is done, use hot water. Stir in the tomato sauce. Return the clams and mussels to the skillet, cover, and warm them, about 1 minute. The risotto should have a flowing consistency, so add hot water if needed.

4. Spoon the risotto and shellfish into six wide soup bowls. Sprinkle with the basil and parsley. Serve hot, with the cheese passed on the side.

Vegetables and Side Dishes

Grandma Josie's Cauliflower and Mushroom Pie

Stuffed Zucchini

Roasted Broccoli Rabe with Olives, Cherry Peppers,
Capers, and Anchovies

Roasted Brussels Sprouts with Onions

Roasted Eggplant Parmigiana

Roasted Portobello Mushrooms with Caramelized Fennel

Stuffed Red Bell Peppers

Giambotta

Potato Croquettes

Potato Pie with Prosciutto and Sopressata

Potato Pie with Scamorza

Roasted Rosemary Potatoes

Fennel and Mushroom Risotto

Grandma Josie's Cauliflower and Mushroom Pie

MAKES 6 TO 8 SERVINGS

This is a great vegetable contribution from my mother-in-law Josephine. She isn't afraid to use a convenience product—such as the biscuit mix she uses here—when it's appropriate. It's a fine side dish, but back in the day when we had meatless Fridays, it was also a nice meatless supper. And Josie still abstains from eating meat on Fridays.

2 tablespoons unsalted butter, at room temperature

1 small head cauliflower, cut into florets

8 ounces white button mushrooms, thinly sliced

1/2 cup olive oil

1 medium yellow onion, finely chopped

1 garlic clove, minced

1/2 teaspoon salt

1/2 teaspoon ground pepper

8 ounces aged provolone, cut into 1/2-inch cubes

1/2 cup dry biscuit mix

2 cups whole milk

1/4 cup freshly grated Parmigiano-Reggiano cheese

1 large egg

2 tablespoons fresh basil chiffonade (see page 8)

1. Preheat the oven to 375°F. Generously grease an 11½ by-8½-inch baking pan with the softened butter.

2. Place a steamer insert in a large saucepan. Add enough cold water to come just short of the insert and bring to a boil over medium heat. Add the cauliflower and cover tightly. Steam until the cauliflower is crisp-tender, about 5 minutes. Add the mushrooms and steam for 2 minutes more. Remove from the heat and uncover.

3. Heat ¼ cup of the oil in medium skillet over medium heat. Add the onion and cook, stirring occasionally, until lightly browned, about 4 minutes. Stir in the garlic and cook until fragrant, about 1 minute. Remove from the heat.

4. Spread the cauliflower and mushrooms in the dish, season with the salt and pepper, and top with the provolone.

5. Whisk the biscuit mix, milk, Parmigiano-Reggiano, egg, basil, and the remaining ¼ cup oil just until combined. Fold in the onion mixture. Pour over the cauliflower mixture in the baking dish.

6. Bake until the pie is lightly browned and a wooden toothpick inserted in the center comes out clean, about 45 minutes. Let stand for 5 minutes at room temperature. Serve hot.

Stuffed Zucchini

MAKES 4 TO 6 SERVINGS

We have Italian-born farmers to thank for bringing the zucchini to America. As with most authentic Italian vegetable recipes, the stuffing lets the zucchini be the star. This is another dish that can do double duty as a side dish or a vegetarian main course.

4 large zucchini
(about 8 ounces each)

¼ cup olive oil,
plus more for greasing

1 small yellow onion,
finely chopped

1 cup Tomato Sauce
(page 100)

½ cup Seasoned Bread
Crumbs (page 14)

Salt and freshly ground
black pepper

¼ cup freshly grated
Parmigiano-Reggiano
cheese

1 large egg, beaten

Chopped fresh flat-leaf
parsley, for garnish

1. Preheat the oven to 450°F. Lightly oil a large baking dish.

2. Cut each zucchini in half lengthwise. With a melon baller or spoon, scoop out the flesh, leaving a ¼-inch-thick shell. Chop the zucchini flesh. Lightly season the zucchini with salt and set aside.

3. Heat the oil in a large skillet over medium heat. Add the onion and cook, stirring occasionally, until lightly browned, about 4 minutes. Stir in the zucchini flesh and cook, stirring often, until tender, about 3 minutes.

4. Stir in the tomato sauce and bring to a boil. Remove from the heat. Stir in the bread crumbs and season to taste with salt and pepper. Transfer to a medium bowl and let cool, stirring often. Add the grated cheese and egg and mix well. Stuff the zucchini with the bread crumb mixture. Arrange the zucchini, stuffed side up, in the prepared baking dish.

5. Bake until the zucchini is tender, about 20 minutes. Sprinkle with the parsley and serve hot from the dish.

Roasted Broccoli Rabe with Olives, Cherry Peppers, Capers, and Anchovies

The cherry peppers give this side dish a nice kick. If you can't find fresh peppers, use the pickled variety or a small red bell pepper, cored and diced. And as much as I love braised broccoli rabe, roasting really is a great way to cook it, too. I think that this method helps smooth out the broccoli rabe's bitterness. Just be sure that it doesn't burn—starting with wet broccoli rabe is the key.

2 bunches broccoli rabe, ends trimmed

$1/2$ cup extra-virgin olive oil

2 garlic cloves, halved

2 fresh or pickled hot red cherry peppers, seeded and coarsely chopped

5 pitted kalamata olives, halved

5 pitted green olives, halved

2 tablespoons drained nonpareil capers, rinsed

2 anchovy fillets in oil, finely chopped

Salt and freshly ground black pepper

1. Preheat the oven to 500°F.

2. Rinse the broccoli rabe thoroughly under cold water. While still wet, transfer the broccoli rabe to a cutting board and cut coarsely with a few chops of the knife. Transfer to a large rimmed baking sheet and toss with ¼ cup of the olive oil

3. Bake until the broccoli rabe begins to wilt, about 4 minutes. Toss the broccoli rabe on the baking sheet to turn it, and roast just until the stems are crisp-tender, about 2 minutes more. Remove from the oven.

4. Meanwhile, heat the remaining ¼ cup oil with the garlic in a large skillet over medium heat, stirring often, until the garlic softens, about 2 minutes. Add the cherry peppers, olives, capers, and anchovies and cook until the peppers soften, about 2 minutes.

5. Add the broccoli rabe to the skillet and cook, tossing occasionally with tongs, to combine the flavors, about 2 minutes. Season to taste with salt and black pepper, taking care to go lightly with the salt because of the saltiness of the olives and anchovy. Transfer to a serving dish. Serve hot.

Roasted Brussels Sprouts with Onions

MAKES 4 SERVINGS

No one made Brussels sprouts like my Aunt Anna. She was roasting them long before you saw it done on television cooking shows. These were the first side dish to disappear from the table at a big dinner—it seemed that she should never make enough to satisfy us. We still make them today, in her honor, and we still go through a big bowl in no time flat.

¼ cup plus 1 tablespoon extra-virgin olive oil

1 medium yellow onion, peeled and diced

Two 10-ounce containers Brussels sprouts, trimmed, rinsed under cold water but not dried

Salt and freshly ground black pepper

1. Preheat the oven to 450°F

2. Heat 1 tablespoon of the oil in a large ovenproof skillet over medium heat. Add the onion and cook, stirring occasionally, until softened, about 3 minutes. Transfer to a plate.

3. Heat the remaining ¼ cup oil in the skillet over medium heat. Add the Brussels sprouts and stir. Transfer to the oven and roast, stirring every 5 minutes or so, until the sprouts are tender and nicely browned, 18 to 22 minutes. If the sprouts brown too quickly, add a few tablespoons of water to the skillet. During the last few minutes, stir in the onion. Season to taste with salt and pepper. Transfer to a serving dish and serve hot.

"I have been eating at Patsy's for over thirty years. Now I must eat gluten-free only. Is it possible that Sal could make my food taste as good as it once did? He did! It is once again sensational! —Danny Aiello

Roasted Eggplant Parmigiana

MAKES 4 TO 6 SERVINGS

For decades, my family has made eggplant Parmigiana the same way that our ancestors made it—with breaded and fried rounds. As good as it is, we don't always have the time for frying, and a lighter more temporary version seemed in order, too. Here's the delicious result, made with roasted eggplant.

2 medium eggplants (about 1¼ pounds each), peeled and cut into ⅓-inch rounds

Olive oil, for brushing

3 cups Tomato Sauce (page 100), heated

8 ounces fresh mozzarella cheese, cut into ½-inch dice

¼ cup freshly grated Parmigiano-Reggiano cheese

1. Position the oven racks in the top third and center of the oven and pre-heat the oven to 450°F. Lightly oil two large rimmed baking sheets.

2. Spread the eggplant rounds on baking sheets, overlapping if needed. Roast until the eggplant is tender, about 20 minutes.

3. Spread ½ cup of the tomato sauce on the bottom of a 9 by 13-inch flameproof baking pan. Place half the eggplant slices in the pan, and top with half the remaining sauce, half the mozzarella, and half the grated Parmigiano-Reggiano. Cover with the remaining eggplant and top with the remaining sauce, mozzarella, and Parmigiano. Spoon about ¼ cup water around the inside edges of the baking pan.

4. Bake, uncovered, until the cheese has melted, about 20 minutes. Remove from the oven. Position a broiler rack about 6 inches from the heat source and preheat the broiler on high. Broil the eggplant Parmigiana until the cheese is lightly browned, 1 to 2 minutes. Serve hot.

Roasted Portobello Mushrooms with Caramelized Fennel

Portobello mushrooms are the steaks of the edible fungi world, with a meaty texture and earthy flavor. Serve these as a side dish for roast pork, or even as a lunch or supper main course with crusty bread.

4 large portobello mushroom caps

¼ cup olive oil, plus more for brushing the mushrooms

Salt and freshly ground black pepper

1 medium fennel bulb, stalks discarded, bulb cored and cut crosswise into thin half-moons

¼ cup chopped fresh basil

½ cup Chicken Stock (page 37), or reduced-sodium store-bought chicken broth or vegetable stock

1. Preheat the oven to 450°F. Lightly oil a large rimmed baking sheet.

2. Place the mushroom caps on the baking sheet and brush with oil. Roast for 10 minutes. Turn them over and continue roasting until tender, 3 to 4 minutes. Season to taste with salt and pepper.

3. Meanwhile, heat ¼ cup of oil in a medium skillet over medium-high heat. Add the fennel and cook, stirring occasionally, until golden brown and tender, about 10 minutes. Stir in the stock and basil and bring to a boil. Season to taste with salt and pepper.

4. Transfer the mushrooms to a cutting board and cut on a slight diagonal into ½-inch-thick slices. Transfer to a serving platter. Pour the fennel sauce over the mushroom slices and serve hot.

Stuffed Red Bell Peppers

MAKES 6 SERVINGS

Many of our family meals have stuffed peppers on the menu. When meat is the main course, we'll serve these lighter, eggplant-filled peppers, which can be served hot or at room temperature. My wife Lisa loves them, perhaps because they are from her Sicilian heritage.

STUFFING

1 pound eggplant

½ cup extra-virgin olive oil, plus more for the pan

1 garlic clove, minced

1 cup canned crushed tomatoes

¼ cup coarsely chopped pitted kalamata olives

2 tablespoons drained nonpareil capers, rinsed

1 anchovy fillet in oil, finely chopped

¼ cup chopped fresh basil

Pinch of sugar

Salt and freshly ground black pepper

3 large red bell peppers

½ cup plain dry bread crumbs

¼ cup freshly grated Parmigiano-Reggiano cheese

Chopped fresh flat-leaf parsley, for garnish

1. Preheat the oven to 425°F. Lightly oil a large rimmed baking sheet.

2. To make the stuffing: Cut the eggplant into ½-inch cubes. Toss the eggplant with 2 tablespoons of the oil on the baking sheet. Roast, stirring occasionally, until tender, about 12 minutes. Remove from the oven.

3. Meanwhile, heat ¼ cup of the oil and the garlic together in a medium skillet over medium heat, stirring occasionally, until golden, about 2 minutes. Stir in the tomatoes, olives, capers, and anchovy and bring to a simmer. Reduce the heat to medium-low and cook for 2 minutes. Stir in the eggplant, basil, and sugar and cook to blend the flavors, about 2 minutes. Season to taste with salt and black pepper. Remove from the heat and cool slightly.

4. Lightly oil a large flameproof baking dish. Cut each pepper in half vertically and remove the cores. Fill each red bell pepper half with the eggplant mixture and place in the dish, stuffing side up. Pour about ⅓ cup water around the pepper halves. Bake until tender, about 20 minutes. Remove from the oven.

5. Position a broiler rack about 6 inches from the heat source and preheat on high. Mix the bread crumbs and grated cheese together in a small bowl and sprinkle over the peppers. Drizzle with the remaining 2 tablepsoons oil. Broil until the crumb topping has browned, 1 to 2 minutes. Sprinkle with the parsley and serve hot from the baking dish.

Giambotta

MAKES 8 TO 12 SERVINGS

Pinch a Neapolitan cook and you will get his or her recipe for this vegetable stew, which utilizes a wide selection of produce simmered together to a tender consistency. There is hardly a vegetable that can't be used, but these are the ones that my family prefers. (The potatoes are parboiled before adding to the tomato sauce to help them cook more evenly, so don't skip this step.) You may as well make a big pot because the leftovers are even better after a day or two of resting and reheating.

¼ cup olive oil

1 large yellow onion, sliced

One 28-ounce can whole plum tomatoes in juice

½ teaspoon dried oregano

¼ teaspoon hot red pepper flakes

8 ounces green beans, cut into 1½-inch lengths

2 medium baking potatoes

1 large red bell pepper, cored, seeded, and cut into ½-inch-wide strips

2 medium zucchini, cut into ½-inch thick half-moons

1 cup thawed frozen green peas

2 tablespoons chopped fresh flat-leaf parsley

Salt and freshly ground black pepper

Freshly grated Parmigiano-Reggiano cheese, for serving

1. Heat the oil in a large saucepan over medium heat. Add the onion and cook, stirring occasionally, until golden, about 4 minutes. Pulse the tomatoes with their juices in a blender a few times until finely chopped but not puréed. Stir into the saucepan with the oregano and red pepper flakes. Bring to a boil. Reduce the heat to medium-low and simmer, stirring occasionally, to blend the flavors, about 10 minutes.

2. Meanwhile, bring a medium saucepan of salted water to a boil over high heat. Add the green beans and cook just until they turn bright green, about 2 minutes. Using a wire strainer, lift and transfer the green beans to a bowl of cold water.

3. Peel the potatoes and cut them into ½-inch cubes. Add the potatoes to the bean cooking water and cook just until they are softened on the outside, about 8 minutes. Using the strainer, transfer the potatoes to the bowl with the green beans. Reserve the cooking water.

4. Drain the green beans and potatoes and add them to the tomato sauce. Simmer for 10 minutes. Stir in the bell pepper, zucchini, peas, and parsley. Season to taste with salt and black pepper. Simmer, adding some of the reserved cooking water if the sauce gets too thick; the giambotta should have a loose, almost soupy, consistency until the vegetables are very tender, about 15 minutes. Serve hot, with the Parmigiano-Reggiano passed on the side.

Potato Croquettes

MAKES ABOUT 16 CROQUETTES

Jerry Stiller and Anne Meara have been eating at Patsy's for decades. In the 1960s, the couple celebrated their first appearance on The Ed Sullivan Show *by dining here afterwards (the studio was only a couple of blocks away; David Letterman taped there, too). We watched their children grow up. When the Stiller family comes for dinner, I know that their daughter Amy will order potato croquettes. Crisp on the outside, creamy on the inside, they are almost too good to be a side dish; you may want to eat them as a main course.*

2 pounds baking potatoes, such as Russets, peeled and cut into 1-inch cubes

2 tablespoons unsalted butter, at room temperature

1 cup whole milk, or as needed

3 cups plain dried bread crumbs

¾ cup grated Parmigiano-Reggiano cheese

¼ cup finely chopped prosciutto

Salt and freshly ground black pepper

4 large eggs

¾ cup (¼-inch) diced fresh mozzarella cheese

Vegetable oil, for deep-frying

Small rosemary sprigs, for serving (optional)

1. Put the potatoes in a large saucepan and add enough cold salted water to cover by 1 inch. Cover and bring to a boil over high heat. Reduce the heat to medium-low and simmer until tender, 20 to 25 minutes. Drain well.

2. Transfer the potatoes to a large bowl. Add the milk and butter. Using a potato masher or handheld electric mixer, mash the potatoes to give them a slightly lumpy consistency. Add 1½ cups of the bread crumbs along with the Parmigiano-Reggiano and prosciutto and mix well. Season to taste with salt and pepper. Beat 2 of the eggs in a small bowl and gradually mix them into the potato mixture. Fold in the mozzarella.

3. Line a baking sheet with waxed paper. Shape the potato mixture into 16 to 18 balls and place on the baking sheet. Flatten each ball slightly with your palm.

4. Beat the remaining 2 eggs in a shallow bowl. Spread the remaining 1½ cups bread crumbs in a pie plate. Coat each croquette in the beaten eggs, roll in the bread crumbs to coat, shake to remove the excess crumbs, and return the croquette to the baking sheet.

5. Preheat the oven to 200°F. Line a rimmed baking sheet with paper towels. Pour enough oil in a large saucepan to come halfway up the sides and heat to 350°F on a deep-frying thermometer. Working in batches, add the croquettes to the oil and deep-fry, turning as needed, until golden brown, about 3 minutes. Using a wire spider or slotted spoon, transfer the croquettes to the paper towel–lined baking sheet and keep warm in the oven while cooking the remaining croquettes, reheating the oil to 350°F between batches. Serve the croquettes hot, topping each with a rosemary sprig, if desired.

Teacher's Pet

My father Joe was raised in Little Italy on Mott Street in New York. One Monday afternoon, when his father Patsy was home and making dinner, Joe's elementary school teacher made a surprise visit to the apartment to discuss some minor classroom indiscretion. Patsy was at the stove making these croquettes, and politely offered one, and then two, to the teacher. Before he knew it, she had eaten the entire pan of croquettes!

When she left, Patsy went straight to Joe and shook his finger in his face, swearing that "If she ever comes back and eats all of my croquettes again, I'm gonna kill you! So you better behave!"

Potato Pie with Prosciutto and Sopressata

MAKES 8 SERVINGS

Every Italian American family has a recipe for potato pie, deliciously seasoned mashed potatoes baked as a side dish. We have two versions, which are quite different. Here is my family's version with three kinds of cheese, and meaty with prosciutto and sopressata.

2 pounds Russet potatoes, peeled and cut into 1½-inch chunks

6 tablespoons (¾ stick) unsalted butter, softened, plus more for the pan

½ cup plain dried bread crumbs

1¼ cups whole milk

¾ cup finely chopped fresh mozzarella cheese

¾ cup freshly grated Parmigiano-Reggiano

¾ cup shredded mild provolone cheese

¼ cup (¼-inch) diced prosciutto

¼ cup peeled and (¼-inch) diced sweet sopressata

2 tablespoons chopped fresh flat-leaf parsley

Salt and freshly ground black pepper

2 large eggs, beaten to blend

1. Put the potatoes in a large saucepan and add enough cold salted water to cover by 1 inch. Cover the saucepan and bring to a boil over high heat. Reduce the heat to medium-low and simmer, covered, until the potatoes are tender, about 20 minutes.

2. Meanwhile, preheat the oven to 425°F. Butter the inside of a 9½-inch-diameter springform pan with 3 inch sides. Coat with ¼ cup of the bread crumbs, and tap out the excess.

3. Drain the potatoes well and transfer to a large bowl. Add 2 tablespoons of the softened butter and the milk. Mash with a potato masher or handheld electric mixer until almost smooth. Fold in the mozzarella, Parmigiano-Reggiano, and provolone cheeses, and the prosciutto, sopressata, and parsley. Season to taste with salt and pepper. Mix in the beaten eggs. Spread in the prepared springform pan. Sift the remaining ¼ cup of the bread crumbs through a coarse-mesh wire strainer over the top of the potato mixture. Dot the top with the remaining softened butter.

4. Put the pan on a baking sheet. Bake until the pie is lightly browned and the mixture looks set in the center when the pan is gently shaken, about 50 minutes. Let stand at room temperature for 20 to 30 minutes to settle. Remove the sides of the pan. Transfer to a serving dish, cut into wedges, and serve warm.

Potato Pie with Scamorza

MAKES 12 TO 16 SERVINGS

My wife's family makes a very big potato pie (really a casserole) that features scamorza, a bulbous pear-shaped cow's milk cheese made in southern Italy (there are domestic versions, too). Some people say scamorza is similar to mozzarella, but it is firmer and melts even more smoothly. Smoked scamorza, which has a light brown skin, is also good in this pie. Look for scamorza at Italian delicatessens and cheese stores. Don't ask me which one I prefer!

---

5 pounds baking potatoes, such as Russets, scrubbed

2¼ cups (5 sticks) unsalted butter: 2 tablespoons softened, 1 pound (4 sticks) sliced into tablespoons, 6 tablespoons (¾ stick) cut into small cubes, plus more softened butter for the baking dish

½ cup plain dried bread crumbs

Salt and freshly ground black pepper

5 large eggs, beaten to blend

1 scamorza cheese (about 12 ounces), cut into ½-inch dice

8 ounces smoked or boiled ham, cut into ½-inch cubes

1. Put the potatoes in a large pot and add enough cold salted water to cover by 1 inch. Cover the pot and bring to a boil over high heat. Reduce the heat to medium-low and simmer until the potatoes are tender, about 30 minutes.

2. Preheat the oven to 350°F. Butter the inside of a 10 by 15-inch baking dish. Coat with ¼ cup of the bread crumbs, and tap out the excess crumbs.

3. Drain the potatoes well. Put the 1 pound of sliced butter into a large bowl. Using a kitchen towel to protect your hands, peel the potatoes and put the hot potatoes into the bowl, letting them melt the butter. Using a potato masher or handheld electric mixer, mash the potato mixture until fairly smooth. Season to taste with salt and pepper. Let the potatoes cool slightly. Gradually stir in the beaten eggs. Fold in the scamorza and ham. Spread in the baking dish. Sprinkle the remaining ¼ cup bread crumbs on top. Scatter the cubed butter over the top and around the inside edges of the pie. Place the dish on a baking sheet.

4. Bake until the top of the pie is golden brown, about 1¼ hours. Let stand at room temperature for 20 to 30 minutes to settle. Serve warm.

Roasted Rosemary Potatoes

MAKES 6 SERVINGS

We serve these with all kinds of meat dishes, from simply grilled chops and steaks to saucy stews. The hardest thing about the recipe is peeling the potatoes!

2 pounds baking potatoes, such as Russets, peeled and cut into ¾-inch cubes

¼ cup olive oil

2 scallions (white and green parts), chopped

2 teaspoons finely chopped fresh rosemary, leaves chopped

Salt and freshly ground black pepper

1. Preheat the oven to 450°F.

2. Toss the potatoes in the oil on a large rimmed baking sheet. Spread the potatoes in a single layer.

3. Roast for 15 minutes. Turn the potatoes over and continue roasting until the potatoes are golden brown and tender, about 10 minutes. Stir in the scallions and rosemary and roast just until the scallions are tender, about 3 minutes more. Season to taste with salt and pepper.

"When you eat at Patsy's, it's like you're with Mia Famiglia. And as you know, Mia Famiglia was an amazing Italian actress from the 1970's! Seriously, great heritage and fantastic food keeps me coming back."
—Al Roker

Fennel and Mushroom Risotto

MAKES 6 SERVINGS

This risotto has earthy cold-weather flavors of fennel and mushrooms. If you like the licorice flavor in fennel, substitute chopped fennel fronds for the basil. There isn't any meat in this except for the chicken stock, and you can easily substitute a vegetable broth to make it completely vegetarian.

3 tablespoons extra-virgin olive oil

1 fennel bulb, quartered, cored, and sliced into thin half-moons

1 medium yellow onion, finely chopped

6 ounces white button mushrooms, thinly sliced

2 cups Arborio rice

6 cups Chicken Stock (page 37) or reduced-sodium store-bought chicken broth

1/2 cup freshly grated Parmigiano-Reggiano cheese (2 ounces), plus more for serving

1/4 cup light cream or half-and-half

3 tablespoons unsalted butter

Salt and freshly ground black pepper

1/3 cup plus 1 tablespoon fresh basil chiffonade (see page 8), for serving

1. Heat the olive oil in a large Dutch oven over medium heat. Add the fennel, mushrooms, and onion and cook, stirring occasionally, until the mushrooms are beginning to brown, about 7 minutes. Add the rice and cook, stirring almost constantly, until it feels heavier in the spoon, about 2 minutes.

2. Meanwhile, bring the stock to a boil in a medium saucepan over high heat. Reduce the heat to very low to keep the stock hot.

3. Stir about ¾ cup of the warm stock into the rice mixture and continue to stir, almost constantly, adjusting the heat so the rice cooks at a steady simmer, until it has almost absorbed all of the liquid, about 2 minutes. Continue adding the liquid, ¾ cup at a time, and stirring until the liquid is absorbed, until the rice is al dente, about 20 minutes. If you run out of broth before the rice is done, use hot water. Stir in the grated cheese, light cream, and butter. Season to taste with salt and pepper.

4. Divide the risotto among six wide soup bowls and sprinkle each with 1 tablespoon of the basil. Serve hot, with more Parmigiano-Reggiano cheese passed on the side.

Holiday Dishes

~~~~

St. Joseph's Bread

Zeppole

Easter Meat and Cheese Pie

Stuffed Leg of Lamb with Prosciutto and Bacon

Easter Bread with Colored Eggs

Pastiera Napolitana (Ricotta and Wheat Berry Cheesecake)

Roast Turkey with Rosemary Gravy

Scognamillo Italian Sausage and Bacon Stuffing

Baccalà Salad

Christmas Escarole

Neapolitan Meatball and Rice Pie

Crown Roast of Pork with Sausage Stuffing

Meatball Lasagna

Struffoli

✦ St. Joseph's Day ✦

Breads and Sweets

March 19 is St. Joseph's Day, a distinctly Italian holiday that celebrates the saint's intervention to end a drought. In our family, it is also commemorated as the name day of my dad, my son, my brother-in-law, and my mother-in-law Josephine. (And I sneak in, too, because Joseph is my middle name.) That's a lot of Josephs.

St. Joseph, the father of Jesus, is especially venerated by Italians from the southern part of the country, such as my ancestors. During a drought in Sicily, the people prayed to St. Joseph for relief. When it came, they celebrated with a feast (of course!) from the harvest. Many Italian families build an altar to St. Joseph, laden with breads and desserts, made from wheat, the most important crop that was saved. Some places in Italy view the date as a kind of Father's Day.

Italian bakeries really go all out for this holiday, and decorated breads are a big item. Some are designed to resemble the saint's staff, which can be as simple as bread bent into a crook to intricately cut breads resembling wheat sheaves. The other hot item that every Italian bakery must sell for St. Joseph's Day is zeppole, a dessert that makes a donut look like diet food. While many people stop by a *pasticceria* to buy baked goods, many wives and mothers make the desserts at home to honor their male head of the household.

St. Joseph's Bread

MAKES 1 LARGE LOAF, ABOUT 12 SERVINGS

St. Joseph gets his own bread on his name day. The recipe and shape changes from village to village in Italy, so there is no single way to make it. This round "crown" braid is easy and impressive. This sweet dough is also used for the Easter Bread with Colored Eggs on page 158.

SWEET DOUGH

1 cup whole milk

½ cup sugar

2 large eggs

1 tablespoon instant (also called bread-machine) yeast

Finely grated zest of 1 lemon

2 teaspoons anise seeds

1½ teaspoons salt

5 cups unbleached all-purpose flour, as needed

6 tablespoons (¾ stick) unsalted butter, cut into tablespoons, at room temperature, plus softened butter for the bowl

1 large egg yolk, beaten with 1 tablespoon whole milk, for the glaze

2 teaspoons sesame seeds

1. To make the sweet dough: Combine the milk, sugar, eggs, yeast, lemon zest, anise seeds, and salt together in the bowl of a heavy-duty stand mixer. Mix with the paddle attachment on low speed until combined. Gradually add 3½ cups of the flour to make a thick batter. One tablespoon at a time, beat in the butter, waiting for the first addition to be absorbed before adding more. Gradually add enough of the remaining flour to make a soft dough that cleans the bowl. Switch to the dough hook and mix on medium-low speed, occasionally pulling down the dough as it climbs up the hook, until the dough is smooth, shiny, and slightly sticky (do not add too much flour), about 8 minutes.

To make the dough by hand: Whisk the milk, sugar, eggs, yeast, lemon zest, anise seeds, and salt together in a large bowl. Gradually stir in 3½ cups of the flour to make a thick batter. One tablespoon at a time, stir in the butter, waiting for the first addition to be absorbed before adding more. Gradually stir in enough of the remaining flour to make a dough that cannot be stirred. Turn the dough out onto a lightly floured work surface and knead, adding more flour as necessary, until the dough is smooth, supple, and slightly sticky (do not add too much flour), about 10 minutes.

2. Butter a large bowl. Gather the dough into a ball. Turn the dough in the bowl to coat it, leaving the dough smooth side up. Cover tightly with plastic wrap and let stand in a warm place until doubled in volume, about 1¼ hours. (Or refrigerate the dough for at least 8 and up to 24 hours.)

3. Line a large rimmed baking sheet with parchment paper. Cut the dough in half. Roll each piece of dough underneath your palms on the work surface into a 22-inch rope, tapering the ends. Place the ropes next to each other and, working from top to bottom, braid them together, leaving the ends loose. Place on the baking sheet and shape into a circle. Where the ends meet, tuck the ends of one braid underneath the opposite ends to complete the braid so no break is visible. Cover loosely with plastic wrap. Let stand in a warm draft-free place until almost doubled in volume, about 1 hour (or 1½ hours for chilled dough).

4. Preheat the oven to 350°F.

5. Brush the braid lightly with the egg glaze and sprinkle with the sesame seeds. Bake until the loaf is golden brown and sounds hollow when tapped on the bottom, about 35 minutes. Let cool completely before slicing.

"I love everything about Patsy's! It's like taking a giant step back in time to the 'Rat Pack' era. My favorite dishes are Patsy's sirloin steak pizzaiola and his Easter meat pie. And I can't leave without a jar of Patsy's famous homemade sauce." —Frank Sinatra, Jr.

Zeppole

Zeppole, a kind of filled doughnut, is by far the most famous of St. Joseph's Day sweets, and for a few days before and after March 19, they line the shelves of Italian bakeries. This is my homemade version, stuffed and topped with pastry cream (or substitute 3 cups of the cannoli cream on page 190 for a delicious variation). You will need a pastry bag with an ½-inch-diameter open star tip.

PASTRY CREAM

3 cups whole milk

$^1/_2$ cup granulated sugar

$^1/_2$ cup all-purpose flour

2 tablespoons cornstarch

6 large egg yolks

$1^1/_2$ teaspoons vanilla extract

Finely grated zest of $^1/_2$ orange

Finely grated zest of $^1/_2$ lemon

ZEPPOLE

$^1/_2$ cup (1 stick) unsalted butter, cut into 8 tablespoons

1 tablespoon granulated sugar

$^1/_4$ teaspoon salt

1 cup all-purpose flour

1. To make the filling: Bring the milk to a simmer in a medium heavy-bottomed saucepan over medium heat. Meanwhile, whisk the flour, sugar, and cornstarch together in a medium heatproof bowl. Whisk the hot milk into the flour. Whisk the yolks in a separate small bowl. Quickly whisk the egg yolks into the hot milk mixture. Return to the saucepan. Bring to a full boil over medium heat, whisking almost constantly. Reduce the heat to medium-low and let boil, whisking, for 1 minute. Strain through a wire fine-mesh sieve into a medium bowl. Whisk in the vanilla, orange zest, and lemon zest. Press a piece of plastic wrap directly on the surface of the pastry cream, pierce a few slits in the wrap with the tip of a knife, and let cool until tepid. Refrigerate until chilled, at least 2 hours or up to 2 days.

2. To make the zeppole: Cut twelve 3-inch squares of parchment paper. Line a large baking sheet with paper towels.

3. Bring 1 cup water, the butter, granulated sugar, and salt to a boil in a medium saucepan over high heat, stirring occasionally to help the butter melt by the time the water boils. Reduce the heat to medium. Add the flour all at once and stir briskly with a wooden spoon to make a stiff dough. Stir until the dough is beginning to film the bottom of the saucepan, about 1½ minutes. Transfer to a large bowl and let cool for 5 minutes. Using an electric mixer set on medium speed, beat in the eggs in four additions, letting the first addition be absorbed into the dough before adding another.

4 large eggs, at room
temperature, beaten
to blend

Vegetable oil, for
deep-frying

12 maraschino cherries
with stems, drained on
paper towels

Confectioners' sugar,
for dusting

4. Fit a large pastry bag with a ½-inch open star pastry tip. Transfer the warm dough to the bag. Pipe a 2¾-inch-diameter circle of dough onto each waxed paper square, with a second ring of dough inside next to the first ring to make a doughnut shape.

5. Pour enough oil into a large wide saucepan to come halfway up the sides and heat over high heat to 360°F. Working in batches without crowding, deep-fry the zeppole until set and the paper squares can be removed with kitchen tongs, about 1 minute. Continue deep-frying, turning halfway through the cooking, until the zeppole are golden brown, about 2½ minutes more. Using a wire skimmer or slotted spoon, transfer the zeppole to the paper towels to drain and cool.

6. To assemble the zeppole: Using a serrated knife, cut each zeppole in half horizontally. Transfer the chilled filling to a large pastry bag fitted with a ½-inch, open star pastry tip. Pipe the filling onto the bottom of each zeppole to fill it, and replace the top. Pipe a rosette of filling into the center of each zeppole to cover the hole, and top with a cherry. Refrigerate until ready to serve. Just before serving, dust confectioners' sugar through a fine-mesh wire sieve over the zeppole.

*"When Frank Sinatra took me to Patsy's in 1977
I knew 2 things: The food and the family making
it would be exemplary. This has not changed
since they opened the door in the mid-40s.
They are not a good Italian Restaurant, they are
one of the best!"—Robert Davi*

◆ Easter Dinner ◆

Easter Meat and Cheese Pie (page 155)

Stuffed Leg of Lamb with Prosciutto and Bacon (page 157)

Steamed Asparagus with Lemon and Butter

Roasted Rosemary Potatoes (page 145)

Easter Bread with Colored Eggs (page 158)

Pastiera Napolitana (page 161)

Easter had a extra meaning for our family because my grandfather's name, Pasquale, derived from *Pasqua*, Italian for "Easter."

For many years, we were closed on Mondays. Easter Sunday was not a day of rest for us, and instead, we celebrated Easter Monday (*La Pasquetta*, or "Little Easter," a bona fide holiday in Italy.) On Sunday, the restaurant cooked and served the holiday dishes that Italian nationals expected: roast baby lamb, spring lamb stew with peas in egg sauce, rabbit in cacciatore sauce, artichokes, asparagus, and of course, *Pastiera*—a kind of ricotta cheesecake with wheat berries in the filling. Native Italians were extremely discriminating clientele, and then, as now, we had to deliver the goods.

Patsy would always order a couple of extra baby lambs to have for our family's Monday feast, but invariably, he would have to roast and serve them on Sunday to satisfy the demand, leaving us empty-handed. The next day, we would have to search around town at butcher shops for replacements.

Easter Meat and Cheese Pie

MAKES 12 TO 14 ANTIPASTO SERVINGS

Up until the mid-1960s, religious Catholics abstained from eating meat during Lent. So, when this pie was served for Easter, meat was making its first appearance in six weeks. We would have this as the first course to a long meal for our Easter Monday dinners. Holiday or not, it is a good choice as a buffet main course, too. The "meat" in this pie is sopressata and prosciutto.

DOUGH

2⅓ cups unbleached all-purpose flour, or as needed

⅔ cup cold water

One ¼-ounce package (2¼ teaspoons) instant (also called bread-machine) yeast

½ teaspoon salt

3 tablespoons unsalted butter, at room temperature

Olive oil, for the bowl

FILLING

2½ pounds whole-milk ricotta cheese

2 ounces sweet sopressata, casing removed, cut into ¼-inch dice

2 ounces hot sopressata, casing removed, cut into ¼-inch dice

4 ounces sliced prosciutto (see page 8), cut into ¼-inch dice

1. For the dough: Combine 1⅔ cups of the flour with the cold water, the yeast, and salt in the bowl of a heavy-duty stand mixer. Mix with the paddle attachment on low speed to make a batter. Add the butter and mix until it is absorbed into the batter and the batter is thinner and stickier. Gradually beat in enough of the remaining flour to make a soft dough that cleans the sides of the bowl. Switch to the dough hook. Knead on medium-low speed until the dough is smooth and elastic, about 8 minutes.

To make the dough by hand. Stir 1⅔ cups of the flour, ⅔ cup water, the yeast and salt together in a large bowl to make a batter. A tablespoon at a time, add the butter, stirring until the butter is completely absorbed into the batter; the batter will be sticky. Gradually stir in enough of the remaining flour to make a dough that is too stiff to stir. Turn the dough out onto a floured surface and knead, adding more flour as needed, to make a soft, supple, and elastic dough, 8 to 10 minutes.

2. Gather the dough into a ball. Place in an oiled medium bowl and turn to coat the dough with oil, leaving the dough smooth side up. Cover tightly with plastic wrap and let stand in a warm, draft-free place until doubled in volume, about 1 hour.

3. To make the filling: Mix the ricotta, sweet and hot sopressata, provolone cheese, grated and diced Parmigiano-Reggiano cheese, and parsley together in a large bowl. Season to taste with salt and pepper. Beat in the eggs and mix well.

½ cup (¼-inch) diced provolone cheese (2 ounces)

4 ounces Parmigiano-Reggiano cheese, ½ cup freshly grated and the remainder cut into ¼-inch dice

3 tablespoons chopped fresh flat-leaf parsley

Salt and freshly ground black pepper

2 large eggs, beaten

Softened butter and flour, for the pan

1 large egg beaten with 1 tablespoon water, for the glaze

4. Preheat the oven to 375°F. Butter and flour the inside of a 9½-inch-diameter springform pan with 3-inch sides.

5. Punch down the dough. Place on lightly floured work surface and cut into two pieces, two-thirds for the bottom and one-third for the top of the pie. Roll out the larger piece of dough into a 16-inch-diameter round. Fit the dough into the pan, letting the excess dough hang over the edge. Add the filling to the pan. Fold the overhanging dough so it barely covers the edges of the filling. Roll out the remaining dough into a 9½-inch-diameter round. Lightly brush the dough around the edge of the filling with the egg glaze. Center the round of dough over the filling. Press the top and bottom crust together. Pierce a small hole in the top of the dough. Brush lightly with the egg glaze. Place the pan on a large rimmed baking sheet.

6. Bake until the crust is golden brown and a small knife inserted into the filling for 5 seconds comes out hot, about 1 hour. Transfer the pie to a wire cooling rack and let stand for 1 hour. Cover with plastic wrap and refrigerate until cooled, at least 3 hours or up to 1 day. Let stand at room temperature for 1 hour before serving.

7. Remove the sides of the pan, cut into wedges, and serve at room temperature.

"Pasquale 'Patsy' Scognamillo's passion was always reflected in the home-style recipes he prepared. The thought of my father, upstairs at his regular table, showing his granddaughters how to make a rocket from a cookie wrapper by rolling it into a cylinder and setting a match to it delights me. This moment, blended with the rich flavors of the delicious food, is etched in my heart forever."
—Nancy Sinatra

Stuffed Leg of Lamb with Prosciutto and Bacon

MAKES 8 SERVINGS

For decades, our first choice for Easter dinner was baby lamb, a meal that had its roots in Naples. Because baby lamb is now so difficult to come by, this is the way that I like to prepare stuffed leg of lamb for the feast. This is no compromise, believe me! You'll have a savory pork and herb filling and a light sauce that truly complements the juicy lamb.

1 boneless leg of lamb, about 6 pounds, trimmed

1 teaspoon salt

1/2 teaspoon freshly ground black pepper

1/4 cup coarsely chopped fresh basil

1 tablespoon finely chopped fresh rosemary

5 garlic cloves, halved lengthwise

2 slices bacon

2 thin slices prosciutto

2 tablespoons olive oil

1 cup Chicken Stock (page 37) or reduced-sodium store-bought chicken broth

1/3 cup dry white wine

2 tablespoons unsalted butter

8 dried bay leaves

1. Preheat the oven to 425°F. Lightly oil a roasting pan.

2. Place the lamb, cut side up, on the work surface, with the long side facing you. Sprinkle with the salt and pepper, followed by the basil, rosemary, and garlic. Place the bacon, running vertically, at opposite short ends of the lamb. Spread the prosciutto out in the center of the lamb to over as much surface as possible. Starting at a short end, roll up the lamb, tucking in the bacon and prosciutto as needed. Tie the lamb crosswise with kitchen twine. Rub the lamb with the oil and place in the pan.

3. Cover the pan with aluminum foil. Roast for 1 hour. Remove the foil and turn the lamb over. Continue roasting, uncovered, for 20 minutes. Remove the pan from the oven. Pour the stock and wine over the lamb and add the butter and bay leaves to the pan. Return the pan to the oven and continue roasting until an instant-read thermometer inserted in the center of the lamb reads 130°F for medium-rare lamb, 5 to 10 minutes more.

4. Transfer the lamb to a carving board and let stand for 15 minutes. Remove and discard the bay leaves and twine. Skim the fat from the pan juices. Bring the juices to a boil in the pan over high heat, scraping up any browned bits in the pan with a wooden spoon; keep warm. Carve the lamb crosswise and transfer to a platter. Pour the pan juices on top and serve hot.

Easter Bread with Colored Eggs

MAKES 1 LARGE LOAF, ABOUT 10 SERVINGS

Every Italian holiday has baked goods specific to the occasion. At Easter, we have this braid with colored Easter eggs on top. (The eggs do not have to be hard-boiled because they will cook in the oven.) This pretty loaf looks like it was made by a bakery, but it is easy to pull off at home.

Sweet Dough (page 149)

6 colored eggs (see Note)

1 large egg yolk beaten with 1 tablespoon whole milk, for glaze

2 teaspoons nonpareils (colored sugar decorations), for garnish

1. Make the Sweet Dough through step 2.

2. Line a large rimmed baking sheet with parchment paper. Divide the dough into thirds. Roll each piece of dough underneath your palms on the work surface into an 20-inch rope, tapering the ends. Line up the ropes next to each other. Starting from the center, braid the ropes to each end, pinching the rope ends together to shape into a tapered loaf. Transfer the braid to the parchment paper–lined-baking sheet. Cover loosely with plastic wrap. Let stand in a warm draft-free place until almost doubled in volume, about 1 hour (or about 1½ hours for chilled dough). During the last 15 minutes of rising, distribute the eggs evenly over the top of the braid, nestling them in the seams.

3. Preheat the oven to 350°F.

4. Brush the braid lightly with the egg glaze and sprinkle with the nonpareils. Bake until the loaf is golden brown and sounds hollow when tapped on the bottom, about 30 minutes. Let cool completely before slicing.

NOTE: To color the eggs, you can use a commercial coloring set, or make your own coloring dip. For each color, combine 1½ cups boiling water and 1 teaspoon white distilled vinegar in a large glass. Tint the liquid as desired with food coloring gel (which has deeper colors than liquid coloring, although you can use liquid). Dip each egg in the coloring mixture, and let stand for at least 2 minutes, or until the desired color is reached. Remove the egg from the coloring mixture and let dry on a wire cooling rack set over a baking sheet.

Pastiera Napolitana (Ricotta and Wheat Berry Cheesecake)

MAKES 10 TO 12 SERVINGS

Easter is the time to make this cross between cheesecake and pie with cooked wheat berries in the filling. (Wheat is a vital symbol in Catholic religion, and some families plant wheat berries at the beginning of Lent to decorate the Easter Dinner table with the small white blossoms.) The dessert is not too sweet; with a distinctive lattice topping, it's the perfect ending to the holiday feast. This must be made a day ahead to cool and set completely, so do not rush it.

1/2 cup soft white wheat berries (see Note)

CRUST

2 1/3 cups all-purpose flour, plus more for kneading

1/2 cup granulated sugar

1/2 cup (1 stick) unsalted butter, cut into 8 tablespoons, at room temperature

2 large eggs, beaten to blend

1/4 cup whole milk

Pinch of salt

FILLING

3 pounds whole-milk ricotta cheese, preferably fresh ricotta

1. The day before serving, put the wheat berries in a medium saucepan and add enough cold water to cover by at least 1 inch. Bring to a boil over high heat. Reduce the heat to medium-low and cover tightly. Simmer, adding boiling water as needed to keep the wheat berries covered, until they are tender, about 1 hour. Drain, rinse under cold running water, and drain again. Pat dry with paper towels and transfer to a bowl. Cover and refrigerate until chilled, at least 1 hour. (The wheat berries can be prepared up to 2 days ahead.)

2. To make the crust: Combine the flour, sugar, butter, eggs, and milk together in the bowl of a heavy-duty stand mixer. Mix on low-speed to form a soft dough that cleans the sides of the bowl. Transfer to a lightly floured work surface. Knead until the dough is smooth, about 1 minute. Shape the dough into a thick disk and wrap in plastic wrap. Refrigerate until the dough is lightly chilled, 30 minutes to 1 hour.

3. To make the filling: Line a large wire sieve with paper towels and place the sieve over a large bowl. Put the ricotta into the sieve and top with more paper towels. Place a plate on top of the ricotta to lightly weigh it. Let stand to drain off some of the whey, about 1 hour.

4. Whisk the sugar and eggs together in a large bowl until thick and pale

1 cup granulated sugar

4 large eggs

2 tablespoons (1/4–inch) diced candied citron

Finely grated zest of 1/2 orange

Confectioners' sugar, for serving

yellow, about 2 minutes. Add the drained ricotta (discard the paper towels), the cooled wheat berries, citron, and orange zest and whisk together to combine.

5. Preheat the oven to 400°F. Lightly butter the inside of a 9½-inch-diameter springform pan with 3 inch sides. Dust the inside of the pan with flour and tap out the excess.

6. Divide the dough for the crust into two pieces, two-thirds for the bottom of the cheesecake and one-third for the top. On a lightly floured work surface, roll out the larger piece of dough into a 17-inch-diameter round. Fit into the pan, being sure the dough fits snugly in the corners. Spread the ricotta filling in the pan. On a lightly floured work surface, roll out the smaller piece of dough into a ⅛-inch-thick round. Using a large knife, cut the dough into ¾-inch-wide strips. Arrange the strips over the filling in a lattice pattern. Trim the bottom dough and fold over the filling. Place the pan on a rimmed baking sheet.

7. Bake until the filling is golden brown and looks set in the center when the pie is gently shaken, about 1 hour and 20 minutes. If the top is browning too quickly, tent it with aluminum foil. Transfer to a wire cooling rack and let cool until tepid. Cover with plastic wrap and refrigerate until completely chilled, at least 8 hours.

8. Remove the sides of the pan. Cut into wedges and serve.

NOTE: Wheat berries, the whole grains of the wheat before it is ground into flour, are sold at natural food stores and many supermarkets. A relatively new variety, soft white wheat berries, are preferred because they take less time to cook than the typical hard red or brown wheat berries. If you can only find hard wheat berries, they will take about 30 minutes longer to simmer to tenderness.

❖ Thanksgiving ❖

Thanksgiving Italian Style

Even our friend and fan, the well-fed comedian Dom DeLuise, always admitted that there was too much food at Thanksgiving. His family had an enormous spread of Italian dishes—lasagna, braciole, ravioli, and the like—in addition to the full contingent of American standards. "Everyone ate the Italian food first, and were too full for the turkey. So we stuck candles in the turkey and used it as the centerpiece."

At my grandparents' home, we stuck with the all-American menu. There wasn't anything Italian about the meal. Patsy or Joe would make a roast turkey like the one on page 000. The only nod to our heritage was the stuffing made with lots of Italian sausage (page 000). Other than that, we could have been Pilgrims. Even dessert was pumpkin pie. I don't think that pumpkin cannoli would be very good.

Estimated Roasting Times (Oven Temperature 325°F)

Here are timings for turkeys from 8 to 24 pounds. There are many variables.

Stuffed Turkey	Time
8–12 pounds	3–3$\frac{1}{2}$ hours
12–14 pounds	3$\frac{1}{2}$–4 hours
14–18 pounds	4–4$\frac{1}{4}$ hours
18–20 pounds	4$\frac{1}{4}$–4$\frac{3}{4}$ hours
20–24 pounds	4$\frac{3}{4}$–5$\frac{1}{4}$ hours

Roast Turkey
with Rosemary Gravy

MAKES 12 TO 16 SERVINGS

My dad Joe makes the Thanksgiving turkey every year. There are a few easy tips to make a great holiday bird. First, fresh turkeys are best. Make a turkey stock from the giblets, and chicken stock to help make a rich and delicious gravy. Cover the breast area with aluminum foil so it doesn't dry out, and remove the foil towards the end of roasting so the skin can brown. Put a little wine and some fresh herbs into your gravy. Be sure to let the roasted turkey stand at room temperature for about 30 minutes so the juices can redistribute themselves before carving. Do these few little things, and you will have a turkey for the gods.

1 whole turkey with giblets, about 18 pounds

TURKEY STOCK

1 tablespoon olive oil

1 medium onion, chopped

1 medium carrot, chopped

1 medium celery rib, chopped

2½ quarts Chicken Stock (page 37) or reduced-sodium store-bought chicken or turkey broth

4 sprigs fresh flat-leaf parsley

1 bay leaf

Scognamillo Italian Sausage and Bacon Stuffing (page 166)

1. Remove the giblets from the turkey and set aside, reserve the liver for another use. Rinse the turkey inside and out with cold running water and pat dry with paper towels. Chop the turkey neck into 2-inch chunks. Pull off the yellow pads of fat from near the tail, cover, and refrigerate. Remove it about 1 hour before roasting.

2. To make the turkey stock: Heat the oil in a large saucepan over medium-high heat. Add the turkey neck, heart, and gizzard and cook, turning occasionally, until well browned, about 10 minutes. Add the onion, carrot, and celery and cook, stirring occasionally, until the onion has softened, about 3 minutes. Add the stock and bring to a boil, skimming off the foam that rises to the surface. Add the parsley and bay leaf. Simmer (but do not boil), skimming off any foam on the surface of the broth, until well flavored, 1½ to 2 hours. Strain the turkey stock, discarding the solids. (The stock can be cooled, covered, and refrigerated for up to 2 days.)

3. Preheat the oven to 325°F. Lightly butter a 9 by 13-inch baking dish.

4. Put the turkey on the work surface, breast side down. Fill the neck cavity with stuffing (do not pack in the stuffing). Using a thin metal skewer, pin the turkey's neck skin to the back. Turn the turkey breast side up. Tie

8 tablespoons (1 stick) unsalted butter, at room temperature, plus more if needed, and softened butter for the baking dish

2 teaspoons salt

1 teaspoon freshly ground black pepper

¾ cup all-purpose flour

½ cup dry white wine

1 tablespoon finely chopped fresh rosemary

the turkey wings to the sides with a loop of kitchen twine. Fill the body cavity with stuffing; do not pack. Cover the exposed stuffing with a piece of aluminum foil. Place the drumsticks in the plastic or metal "hock lock" at the turkey's tail, or tie the drumsticks together with kitchen twine. Place any remaining stuffing in the baking dish, cover with aluminum foil, and refrigerate.

5. Place the turkey, breast side up, on a rack in a large metal pan. Rub all over with the softened butter, and season all over with the salt and pepper. Tightly cover the breast area with aluminum foil. Pour 2 cups of the turkey stock into the bottom of the pan and add the reserved turkey fat.

6. Roast the turkey, basting all over every 45 minutes with the juices on the bottom of the pan (lift up the foil to reach the breast area), until a meat thermometer inserted in the meaty part of the thigh (but not touching a bone) reads 180°F degrees and the stuffing is at least 160°F, about 4¼ hours. (See Estimated Roasting Times, on page 163.) Remove the foil during the last hour to allow the skin to brown. When the pan drippings evaporate and form a brown film in the bottom of the pan, add 1 cup water, adding more water as needed throughout the roasting period.

7. Transfer the turkey to a large serving platter and let it stand for 30 to 45 minutes before carving. Increase the oven temperature to 350°F. Drizzle ½ cup of turkey stock over the stuffing in the casserole, cover, and bake until heated through, about 30 minutes.

8. Meanwhile, to make the gravy: Pour the drippings from the roasting pan into a heatproof glass bowl or measuring cup. Let stand 5 minutes; then skim off and reserve the clear yellow fat that rises to the top. Measure ¾ cup fat, adding melted butter, if needed. Add enough turkey broth to the skimmed drippings to make 8 cups total.

9. Place the roasting pan over two stove burners on low heat and add the rendered turkey fat. Add the flour and whisk, scraping up the browned bits on the bottom of the pan with a whisk. Cook until the flour is lightly browned, about 2 minutes. Whisk in the wine and rosemary, followed by the turkey broth. Cook, whisking often, until the gravy thickens and reduces to the consistency of heavy cream, about 10 minutes. Season with salt and pepper. Transfer the gravy to a warmed gravy boat. Carve the turkey and serve the gravy alongside.

Scognamillo Italian Sausage and Bacon Stuffing

MAKES ABOUT 3 QUARTS STUFFING, 16 TO 20 SERVINGS

It's not Thanksgiving without our sausage and bacon stuffing, made every year by my dad Joe. It is best to make the stuffing fresh and use it warm, as cold stuffing takes longer to cook inside of the bird. Also, remember that you will not be able to fit all of the stuffing in the bird, and there will always be leftover dressing to bake on the side.

2 tablespoons olive oil

2½ pounds sweet Italian sausages, casing removed

12 ounces bacon, cut into 1-inch pieces

One 1-pound loaf day-old Italian bread (about 1 pound)

1 cup freshly grated Parmigiano-Reggiano cheese

3 large eggs, beaten to blend

½ cup seedless raisins

½ cup pine nuts

¼ cup chopped fresh flat-leaf parsley

1 tablespoon finely chopped sage and rosemary

Salt and ground pepper

1½ cups Chicken Stock (page 37) or reduced-sodium chicken broth, as needed

1. Heat the oil in a large skillet over medium heat. Add the sausage and cook, breaking up the sausage into small pieces with the side of a spoon, until browned and shows no sign of pink, about 8 minutes. Transfer the sausage and any fat to a large bowl.

2. Add the bacon to the skillet. Cook over medium heat, stirring often, until browned and crisp, about 8 minutes. Using a slotted spoon, transfer the bacon to the sausage. Discard the bacon fat.

3. Cut the bread into ¾-inch cubes. Add the bread cubes, grated cheese, raisins, pine nuts, and parsley and stir to combine. Season to taste with salt and pepper. Mix in the eggs and enough of the broth to make a moist, but not wet, mixture.

4. Use immediately as a turkey stuffing. Any leftover stuffing can be spread in a buttered baking dish, covered with aluminum foil, and refrigerated for up to 8 hours. Just before baking, uncover the dish and drizzle the stuffing with about ½ cup stock. Cover again and bake in a preheated 350°F oven for 20 minutes. Remove the foil and continue baking until the top is golden brown and slightly crisp, 15 to 20 minutes more. Serve hot.

◆ Feast of the Seven Fishes ◆

Baccalá Salad (page 168)

Insalata di Frutti di Mare (page 29)

Shrimp Casino (page 20)

Fried Cod Fritters (page 86)

Mussels Marinara (page 18)

Octopus Affogati with Linguine (page 95)

Christmas Escarole (page 169)

Struffoli (page 179)

One of the most important feasting days is actually a night—Christmas Eve. To Southern Italians, this means one thing—The Feast of the Seven Fishes, an incredible meal with seafood as the star.

For many years, many religious holidays had abstinence rules, and you were not allowed to eat meat or dairy products on Christmas Eve in order to spiritually prepare yourself for the coming holy day. No meat and dairy? No problem. The Italians just served up lots of seafood (at least seven different dishes), cooked or fried in oil instead of butter.

The reason why seven fishes are served is unclear. Some people believe that it is simply because the number seven has taken on a cosmic meaning (as in "lucky seven"). The number shows up often in the Catholic faith, with the Seven Sacraments as an example, and it is mentioned many times in the Bible (consider the Seven Deadly Sins, or that God created the world in seven days). For our family, the number of seafood items we serve is flexible, and it is rarely as few as seven.

Baccalà Salad

Marinated baccalà salad is a must for the Seven Fishes Christmas Eve Feast. The fish is soaked to remove the salt for no less than three (or four, if you have time) days, so plan ahead. Buy relatively thick snowy white fillets—if the fish looks yellowish, pass it up.

2 pounds
skinless salt cod fillets

¹/₃ cup plus 1 tablespoon
fresh lemon juice

2 tablespoons finely
chopped fresh basil

1 garlic clove, finely chopped

¹/₄ cup extra-virgin olive oil

¹/₂ cup coarsely chopped
pitted kalamata olives

Salt and freshly ground
black pepper

1. Cut each fillet into three or four pieces. Rinse the surface salt off the cod under cold running water. Place the cod in a large bowl and cover with cold water. Cover and refrigerate, changing the water at least twice a day, until looks it fully rehydrated, at least 3 and up to 4 days.

2. Drain the cod well. Cut into 3-inch pieces and put them in a large saucepan. Add enough cold water to cover by 1 inch. Bring to a boil over high heat. Reduce the heat to medium and cover. Simmer until the fish flakes easily with a fork, 15 to 20 minutes. Drain the cod in a colander. Transfer to a bowl of cold water and let cool for about 10 minutes.

3. Meanwhile, whisk the lemon juice, basil, and garlic together in a large bowl. Gradually whisk in the oil.

4. Drain the cod and flake the fish with a fork. Add the flaked cod and olives to the lemon dressing and toss to coat. Season lightly to taste with salt and pepper. Cover and refrigerate at least 1 hour and up to 1 day before serving. Serve chilled or at room temperature.

Christmas Escarole

Another dish that is always served on Christmas Eve is braised escarole. This bitter green is cooked with a little garlic as a side dish throughout the year, but during the holidays, it is dressed up with pine nuts, olives, capers, and raisins, with anchovies as the required fish element.

2 pounds escarole, tough ends trimmed, coarsely chopped

1/2 cup plus 1 tablespoon olive oil

4 garlic cloves, coarsely chopped

1/2 cup dark raisins

1/3 cup drained nonpareil capers, rinsed

1/4 cup pine nuts, toasted (see page 103)

1/4 cup coarsely chopped pitted kalamata olives

3 anchovy fillets in oil, finely chopped

Salt and freshly ground black pepper

1/2 cup Seasoned Bread Crumbs (page 14)

1. Wash the escarole well in several changes of cold water to remove all the grit. Place the wet escarole in a large saucepan and heat over high heat until steaming. Cover tightly and reduce the heat to low. Cook until the escarole has completely wilted, about 10 minutes. Drain well.

2. Heat 1/2 cup of the oil and the garlic together in a large skillet over medium heat, stirring often, until the garlic is golden, about 2 minutes. Stir in the raisins, capers, pine nuts, olives, and anchovies. Add the escarole, mix well, and reduce the heat to medium-low. Cook, stirring often, until the escarole is very tender, about 20 minutes. Season to taste with salt and pepper. Remove from the heat and let stand for 30 minutes to 2 hours. Just before serving, reheat over medium heat, stirring often, until hot, about 3 minutes.

3. Position a broiler rack 6 inches from the heat source and preheat the broiler to high. Spread the escarole in a flameproof baking dish. Sprinkle with the bread crumbs and drizzle with the remaining oil. Broil until the crumbs are toasted, about 1 minute, watching carefully to avoid burning. Serve hot.

◆ Christmas Dinner ◆

Eggplant Caponata (page 21)
Neapolitan Meatball and Rice Pie (page 171)
Meatball Lasagna (page 175)
Crown Roast of Pork with Sausage Stuffing (page 173)
Giambotta (page 140)
Roasted Brussels Sprouts with Onions (page 133)
Roasted Broccoli Rabe with Olives, Cherry Peppers, Capers,
and Anchovies (page 130)
Yummy Butter Cookies (page 185)
Fried Bows (page 186)
Anise Biscotti (page 182)
Struffoli (page 179)

Christmas was a very special day to us because it was the one holiday for which we always closed, and the entire family could be together. Dinner was actually lunch, starting about 1 P.M. after everyone returned from Mass. It was a meal eaten in waves, not courses.

First, a huge antipasti spread with salami, cheeses, pickled vegetables, and always Grandma's caponata with toasted bread, was spread out. You could fill up on that alone! Next came a pasta course with manicotti or lasagna augmented with meatball and rice pie. To "open up our appetites" for the next onslaught of food, my grandfather would pass around sticks of fresh fennel to munch on. And then came a roast of some kind, and an array of side dishes.

Dessert was always a beautiful selection of cookies from various women in the family, each presenting their specialty. Even if we were too full, a platter of struffoli, the tiny fried dough balls stuck together with honey syrup, was brought out to nibble at while we sipped our last cup of coffee. This was my favorite part of the meal because my grandfather would make me feel like a grown-up by giving me a tiny sip of the Sambuca that he always drank with his espresso.

Neapolitan Meatball and Rice Pie

MAKES 10 TO 12 FIRST-COURSE SERVINGS

2 cups long-grain rice

Salt

4 tablespoons (½ stick) unsalted butter; 1 tablespoon softened, 3 tablespoons cut into small cubes

½ cup plain dried bread crumbs

7 cups Tomato Sauce (page 100)

½ recipe Meatball-tini, (page 13)

1 cup (½-inch) cubed fresh mozzarella cheese

½ cup freshly grated Pecorino Romano cheese

1 cup thawed frozen green peas

2 tablespoons finely chopped fresh flat-leaf parsley

2 tablespoons finely chopped fresh basil

Freshly ground black pepper

2 large eggs, beaten to blend

½ cup freshly grated Pecorino Romano cheese, for serving

½ cup fresh basil chiffonade (see page 8), for serving

Patsy used to make this for my grandmother Concetta's name day and other family holidays. We enjoyed it in small slices as a first course, but you can have it as a main dish as long as you serve something light, like salad, as the side dish. You might ask why we don't use short-grain Italian rice here. It is simply because Grandpa couldn't get imported rice, and we got used to making it with the long-grain American variety.

1. Bring a large pot of salted water to a boil over high heat. Add the rice and cook (like pasta) until al dente, about 17 minutes. Drain, but do not rinse. Transfer to a large bowl and let cool, stirring often.

2. Preheat the oven to 425°F. Butter the inside of a 9½-inch-diameter springform pan with 3-inch sides. Coat with ¼ cup of the bread crumbs, tapping out the excess.

3. Add 4 cups of the tomato sauce, the mini meatballs, mozzarella, ½ cup of the Pecorino Romano, the peas, parsley, and 2 tablespoons of the basil to the rice and mix thoroughly. Season to taste with salt and pepper. Gradually stir in the eggs. Spread in the pan. Sift the remaining ¼ cup bread crumbs through a wire strainer over the top of the rice mixture. Dot with the cubed butter. Place the pan on a baking sheet. Bake until the pie is lightly browned and looks set in the center when the pan is shaken lightly, about 50 minutes. Let stand at room temperature for 20 to 30 minutes.

4. To serve, heat the 3 cups of remaining tomato sauce. Remove the sides of the pan. Cut the pie into wedges and transfer each to a salad plate. Spoon the tomato sauce over each and sprinkle with basil and Pecorino Romano. Serve warm.

Crown Roast of Pork with Sausage Stuffing

MAKES 8 TO 12 SERVINGS

My dad likes to make a big roast for the holidays, and crown roast of pork is one of his specialties. It is an impressive roast, made from two pork loins tied together in a large round. Be sure to order it ahead from your butcher. The open center of a crown roast is perfect for a stuffing, and we usually use our Scognamillo Italian Sausage and Bacon Stuffing on page 166). For a lighter alternative, you can fill the center with sautéed seasonal vegetables or even a big batch of Christmas Escarole on page 169.

One 8½–pound crown roast of pork, with 12 to 14 ribs

2 tablespoons olive oil, plus more for the baking dish

2 teaspoons finely chopped fresh sage

2 teaspoons finely chopped fresh rosemary

1 teaspoon salt

½ teaspoon freshly ground pepper

Scognamillo Italian Sausage and Bacon Stuffing (page 166)

½ cup dry white wine

2 recipes Quick Brown Sauce (page 56) (about 3½ cups

1. Preheat the oven to 450°F. Lightly oil a 9 by 13-inch baking dish.

2. Place the roast in a roasting pan just large enough to hold it comfortably. In a small bowl, combine the sage, rosemary, salt, and pepper. Brush the roast with the oil, then season all over with the herb mixture. Le the roast stand at room temperature for 30 minutes.

3. Loosely fill the center of the roast with some of the stuffing. Transfer the remaining stuffing to the oiled baking dish, cover with aluminum foil, and refrigerate. Cover the exposed stuffing in the roast with foil. Cover each of the bone tips with a small piece of foil.

4. Bake the roast for 10 minutes. Reduce the oven temperature to 325°F. Cook until a meat thermometer inserted in the thickest part of the roast, without touching a bone, reads 145°F, about 2 hours. During the last 15 minutes of roasting time, remove the foil from the stuffing and bone tips so they will brown. Using a wide spatula (or a rimless baking sheet or even the flat bottom of a tart pan), transfer the roast to a warmed serving platter. Tent with aluminum foil and let stand for 20 minutes before carving.

5. Increase the oven temperature to 425°F. Bake the reserved stuffing until heated through, about 20 minutes.

6. Meanwhile, discard any fat in the roasting pan. Place the pan on the stovetop over medium heat. Add the wine and bring to a boil, scraping up the browned bits in the pan with a wooden spoon. Stir in the brown sauce and bring to a simmer. Reduce the heat to low and cook, stirring often, until slightly reduced, about 5 minutes. Season to taste with salt and pepper. Divide the sauce between two sauceboats.

7. Using a long, sharp knife, starting at the center of the stuffing, cut the roast into 1-rib servings. Transfer the pork and stuffing to dinner plates, and serve, with the sauce passed on the side.

Tony Bennett's Mom's Secret Ingredient

At Tony Bennett's eighty-fifth birthday, the main course was his mother's lasagna, which had a hint of cinnamon in the sauce. The guests were buzzing about the "unusual" seasoning. I mentioned to Patricia, his sister-in-law, that I thought that the spice would have been nutmeg, not cinnamon. She whispered in my ear, "It should have been. The old girl made us swear never to give out the recipe, so we changed it."

Meatball Lasagna

Our lasagna makes an appearance at just about every Scognamillo family event, from Christmas dinners to birthday parties. When I made this on Martha Stewart's television show, we had so many customers asking for it that we sold out every night for three months. Somewhat different than the one you are probably familiar with, it is cooked with a minimum of tomato sauce so the layers remain distinct when the lasagna is cut, and then it is topped with the sauce for serving. We insist on fresh pasta, so order it ahead of time from your source, or make according to the instructions on page 101. With four layers of mini meatballs, mozzarella, sausage, and ricotta, this very special lasagna is impressively thick, so you must use a pan that is at least 3 inches deep.

1¼ pounds sweet
Italian sausage

3 pounds fresh
lasagna sheets

Olive oil, for the pan

7 cups Tomato Sauce
(page 100)

1 recipe Meatball–tini
(page 13)

1 cup freshly grated Pecorino
Romano cheese, plus more
for serving

1 cup chopped fresh basil
chiffonade (see page 8)

2 pounds fresh mozzarella
cheese, cut into ½-inch
cubes

2 pounds whole–milk
ricotta cheese

1 large egg, beaten

1. Position a broiler rack about 6 inches from the heat source and preheat the broiler on high. Broil the sausages, turning often, until browned and cooked through, 12 to 15 minutes. Transfer to a carving board and let cool. Cut crosswise into ¼-inch rounds.

2. Bring a large pot of salted water to a boil over high heat. Add the pasta and cook (the water does not have to return to a boil) according to the manufacturer's directions until barely tender. (If using the Basic Egg Pasta on page 101, just until barely tender, about 1 minute.) Do not overcook. Drain and transfer to a large bowl of cold water.

3. Preheat the oven to 450°F. Lightly oil a 9 by 13 by 3-inch deep-dish lasagna pan.

4. Spread ½ cup of the tomato sauce in the bottom of the pan. Cut 8 of the lasagna sheets to yield 16 strips about 8 inches long. (Any pasta trimmings can be used in the center layers of the lasagna.) Using your fingers, smear a tablespoon of the tomato sauce all over a pasta strip. Fit the strip diagonally into a corner of the pan, with about 2 inches of each strip hanging over the pan, and fitting the rest of the strip along the side and bottom of the pan. Repeat with the other 3 corners of the pan.

Place the remaining strips around the perimeter of the pan, first smearing each lightly with tomato sauce, with about 2 inches hanging over the pan, and fitting the remaining lengths along the side and bottom of the pan. Lay 2 full strips, cut to fit, horizontally into the bottom of the pan.

5. For the meatball layer, mix the meatballs, ¼ cup of the Pecorino Romano, and ¼ cup of basil in a medium bowl. Spread evenly in over the pasta layer. Spoon 1 cup of the tomato sauce over the meatball mixture. Top with a horizontal layer of pasta sheets, cut to fit, to cover.

6. For the sausage layer, in the same bowl, mix the sliced sausage and ¼ cup of the Pecorino Romano. Spread evenly over the pasta layer. Spoon 1 cup of the tomato sauce over the sausage mixture. Top with a horizontal layer of pasta sheets, cut to fit, to cover.

7. For the mozzarella layer, in the same bowl, mix the mozzarella, ¼ cup of the Pecorino Romano, and ¼ cup of basil. Spread evenly over the pasta layer. Spoon 1 cup of the tomato sauce over the mozzarella mixture. Top with a horizontal layer of pasta sheets, cut to fit, to cover.

8. For the ricotta layer, in the same bowl, mix the ricotta, the remaining ¼ cup Pecorino Romano, and the egg. Spread evenly over the pasta layer. Spoon 1 cup of the tomato sauce over the ricotta mixture.

9. Top with a final layer of pasta sheets, leaving a ½-inch border around the edges of the pan. Brush the top layer of pasta and the overhanging pasta strips with the remaining tomato sauce in the pie plate. Fold the strips into the pan, trimming as needed, so you end up with a neat border (resembling a picture frame) around the edge of the lasagna. Oil one side of a 9 by 13-inch sheet of parchment paper. Place, oiled side down, on the lasagna. Cover the pan tightly with a double layer of aluminum foil. Cover and refrigerate the remaining tomato sauce.

10. Place the pan in a large roasting pan. Place both pans in the oven and add enough hot water in the larger pan to come about halfway up the sides. Bake for about 2 hours, or until an instant-read thermometer inserted in the center reads 160°F.

11. Let the lasagna stand at room temperature for about 20 minutes. Reheat the tomato sauce. To serve, cut into squares and transfer each to a dinner plate. Top with a spoonful of the tomato sauce and a sprinkle of the remaining basil. Serve hot, with more Pecorino Romano passed on the side.

Struffoli

MAKES 6 TO 8 SERVINGS

Christmas dinner is over. You have been eating for about twenty-four hours straight, starting with the Feast of Seven Fishes the night before. Dessert has come and gone, and you swear that you cannot eat another bite. And then, one of your aunts or cousins brings out a plate of her homemade struffoli, little balls of fried dough, glazed with honey, and you find that you can nibble just a bit longer. These go down very easily with an espresso or a glass of sweet wine, such as Marsala.

2 cups all-purpose flour, sifted

1/2 teaspoon baking powder

1/2 teaspoon salt

3 large eggs

1/2 teaspoon vanilla extract

Vegetable oil, for frying and oiling the serving dish

1 cup honey

Nonpareils (colored sugar sprinkles), for garnish

Maraschino cherries, for garnish

1. Combine the flour, baking powder and salt in a medium bowl. Make a well in the center and, one at a time, stir in the eggs. Add the vanilla and mix well to make a soft dough. Knead on a lightly floured surface until smooth, about 5 minutes. Wrap the dough in plastic wrap and let stand at room temperature for 30 minutes.

2. Working with one half at a time, roll the dough into a 1/4-inch-thick rectangle. Cut the dough into 1/2-inch-wide strips. Roll each strip under the palms of your hands on the work surface to make long pencil-thick ropes. Cut the ropes into 1/4-inch pieces. Transfer the dough pieces to a large rimmed baking sheet.

3. Line another large rimmed baking sheet with a few layers of paper towels. Pour enough oil into a large wide saucepan to come halfway up the sides and heat over high heat to 350°F. Working in batches without crowding, add the dough pieces and deep-fry, turning them as needed, until golden brown, about 3 minutes. Using a wire skimmer or slotted spoon, transfer to the paper towel–lined baking sheet.

4. Lightly oil a round serving dish. Heat the honey in a large skillet over medium heat until fluid. Add the balls and stir until completely coated. Spoon the balls onto the baking sheet. Garnish with the nonpareils and cherries. Let cool.

Desserts

〰

Anise Biscotti

Panettone Bread Pudding

Yummy Butter Cookies

Fried Bows

Panna Cotta with Raspberry Sauce

Chocolate and Hazelnut Gelato

Strawberries with Cannoli Cream

Grandma Josie's Cream Puffs

Rice Pudding Tart with Dried Cherries

Peach Crostata

Apple Fritters

Anise Biscotti

We keep desserts simple at Patsy's. I think it is because my father worked at a bakery starting when he was six years old, where he learned how much customers love the Old World classics like biscotti and cannoli. (There is a great story about his boss making him whistle all day long so he could tell that the kid wasn't eating up the profits.) Many of our guest's meals are finished with a plate of these anise biscotti and an espresso.

---

3 cups all-purpose flour, plus more for shaping the dough

2 teaspoons baking powder

Pinch of salt

1¼ cups granulated sugar

½ cup (1 stick) unsalted butter, at room temperature

3 large eggs plus 1 large egg yolk

1½ teaspoons honey

1 teaspoon anise extract

Confectioners' sugar, for sifting

1. Preheat the oven to 350°F. Line a large rimmed baking sheet with parchment paper.

2. Whisk the flour, baking powder, and salt together. Beat the butter and sugar together in a large bowl in the bowl of a heavy-duty stand mixer with the paddle attachment until the mixture is light in color and texture, about 3 minutes. One at a time, beat in the whole eggs, followed by the egg yolk, honey, and anise extract. With the mixer on low speed, gradually add the flour mixture to make sticky soft dough.

3. Turn out the dough onto a floured work surface and divide into thirds. Shape each portion of dough, coating with flour as necessary to keep it from sticking, into an 11-inch-long log. Transfer the logs to the baking sheet, spacing them evenly apart. Using floured hands, pat the top of each log to flatten it into a ½-inch thickness.

4. Bake until the loaves are golden brown and feel firm, about 25 minutes. Let cool on the baking sheets for about 20 minutes. Transfer the loaves to a cutting board. Using a serrated knife, cut the loaves crosswise into ½-inch-thick slices.

5. Position a rack about 8 inches from the heat source and preheat the broiler on high. Working in batches, spread the biscotti, cut sides up, on the baking sheet and broil, watching carefully to avoid burning, until lightly browned, about 1 minute. Remove from the broiler, turn the biscotti over, and return to the broiler to brown the other sides. Transfer to wire cooling racks and let cool completely.

Panettone Bread Pudding

MAKES 6 TO 8 SERVINGS

Panettone (a golden sweet bread flavored with dried fruit) is a very special holiday gift, and we get quite a few loaves at Christmastime. This creamy pudding is one of my favorite ways to enjoy it.

4 large eggs, beaten

2 cups whole milk

1 cup light cream or half-and-half

½ cup orange-flavored liqueur (Grand Marnier)

½ cup sugar

4 tablespoons (½ stick) unsalted butter, melted, plus softened butter for the baking dish

1 teaspoon vanilla extract

1 teaspoon ground cinnamon

Finely grated zest of 1 large orange

¼ teaspoon salt

One 1-pound panettone bread, cut into 1-inch pieces

WHIPPED CREAM

1 cup heavy cream

2 tablespoons sugar

½ teaspoons vanilla extract

1. To make the pudding: Whisk the eggs in a large bowl. Add the milk, light cream, liqueur, sugar, butter, vanilla, cinnamon, zest, and salt. Add the panettone and stir to evenly moisten the bread cubes. Let stand until the bread soaks up most of the liquid, about 15 minutes,

2. Meanwhile, preheat the oven to 350°F. Lightly butter a 9 by 13-inch baking dish.

3. Spread the bread mixture evenly in the baking dish. Place the pan in a larger pan. Place the pans in the oven and add enough hot water to come halfway up the sides of the larger pan. Bake until a knife inserted in the center of the pudding comes out clean, about 50 minutes. Remove from the oven and remove the baking dish from the larger pan. Let cool for 15 to 30 minutes.

4. To make the whipped cream: Whip the cream, sugar, and vanilla with an electric handheld mixer on high speed in a chilled medium bowl until the mixture forms soft peaks. Cover and refrigerate until ready to serve.

Yummy Butter Cookies

MAKES 10 DOZEN COOKIES

My wife Lisa loves to bake, especially at Christmas when she gets together with her mother Josephine to make a huge assortment of beautiful cookies. They always make these simple butter cookies. One of their main attractions is that the kids in the family can get involved rolling the dough into balls. In fact, we call these "yummy cookies" because when our son Joseph was about two, he was "helping" Lisa make the cookies when she noticed that the dough was disappearing. Of course, Joey had been eating the raw dough. His verdict? "It was yummy!"

1 pound (4 sticks) unsalted butter, at room temperature

1¼ cups sugar

6 large egg yolks

2 teaspoons vanilla extract

5 cups all-purpose flour

1 teaspoon baking powder

One 4-ounce container red or green candied cherries, cut into ½-inch pieces

1. Beat the butter and sugar together in the bowl of a heavy-duty stand mixer on high speed until light in color and texture, about 3 minutes. One at a time, beat in the egg yolks, followed by the vanilla. Whisk the flour and baking powder together. With the mixer on low speed, gradually add the flour mixture and mix to make a stiff dough. Gather up the dough into a thick disk. Wrap in plastic wrap, refrigerate, and chill and firm slightly, at least 2 and up to 8 hours.

2. Position the racks in the top third and center of the oven and preheat the oven to 350°F. Line two baking sheets with parchment paper.

3. Using a rounded teaspoon for each cookie, roll the dough between your palms into 1-inch balls. Place the balls about 1 inch apart on the baking sheets. Press a cherry piece in the center of each cookie.

4. Bake, switching the position of the baking sheets from top to bottom and front to back halfway through baking, until the cookies are very lightly browned, 15 to 18 minutes. Let cool on the sheets for 3 minutes, then transfer to wire cooling racks to cool completely. (The cookies can be stored in an airtight container at room temperature for up to 1 week.)

Fried Bows

MAKES 8 DOZEN COOKIES

It seems that every country has a tradition of fried cookies coated in confectioners' sugar, and Italy has its version, too. These have been on our family's Christmas cookie tray for as long as we can remember. You'll need a ravioli or pizza wheel to cut the strips. These are best eaten the day they are made.

3½ cups all-purpose flour, or as needed

1 tablespoon baking powder

¼ teaspoon salt

4 tablespoons (½ stick) unsalted butter, at room temperature, cut into tablespoon-size pieces

1 cup granulated sugar

5 large eggs, beaten, at room temperature

1 tablespoon vanilla extract

Vegetable oil, for deep-frying

Confectioners' sugar, for sifting

1. Whisk 3 cups of the flour, baking powder, and salt together in a medium bowl. Add the butter and rub it into the dry ingredients with your fingertips until the mixture looks crumbly. Make a well in the center of the flour mixture, and add the sugar, eggs, and vanilla. Using a spoon, gradually stir into the flour mixture to make a moist dough.

2. Transfer the dough to a floured work surface. Knead, adding as much of the remaining flour as needed, to make a soft, tacky dough that barely sticks to the work surface, about 3 minutes. Transfer to a floured work surface and cover with an inverted bowl for 10 minutes. Knead for about 1 minute more, adding a bit more flour, if needed. Cover the dough and let stand for at least 10 and up to 30 minutes. The dough will still feel tacky, but should be firm enough to roll out; knead in more flour, if needed.

3. Pour enough oil into a large saucepan to come halfway up the sides, and heat over high heat to 360°F on a deep-frying thermometer. Line a large baking sheet with a double layer of paper towels.

4. Divide the dough into quarters. Working with one-quarter at a time, roll out the dough into a 6 by 22-inch rectangle about ⅟₁₆-inch thick. Using a ravioli cutter, cut into ¾-inch-wide strips. Loosely tie each strip into an overhand knot, with the knot in the middle of each strip. Place on a large baking sheet. Working in batches, without crowding, deep-fry the cookies, turning occasionally, until golden brown and crisp, about 2½ minutes. Using a wire skimmer or slotted spoon, transfer the cookies to the paper towel–line baking sheet to drain. Immediately sift confectioners' sugar through a wire sieve over the warm cookies. Repeat with the remaining dough. (The cookies can be stored, uncovered, at room temperature, for up to 12 hours.) Just before serving, sift a fresh layer of confectioners' sugar over the cookies.

Everybody's a Critic

Rapper Puff Daddy is another performer who has enjoyed many meals here. He got very close to my aunt Anna, who was always at the front desk running the ship. Once she asked him for his autograph for her grandchildren. She offered, "They love your music, but I like Frank and Tony a lot better."

He thought this bald-faced honesty was hilarious. When she died, he send two dozen roses to the restaurant, with the card, "Rest in Peace, Anna—my best critic."

Panna Cotta with Raspberry Sauce

MAKES 6 SERVINGS

Panna cotta means "cooked cream," but it isn't really cooked, just heated to dissolve the gelatin. I like the combination of vanilla cream with tart raspberry sauce. One of the great things about panna cotta (besides its flavor and texture) is that it must be made a few hours before serving, so you can give a dinner party knowing that dessert is out of the way and in the fridge.

PANNA COTTA

Vegetable oil,
for the ramekins

1/2 cup whole milk

1 tablespoon unflavored gelatin powder (not quite an entire packet)

2 1/2 cups heavy cream

1/3 cup plus 1 tablespoon sugar

2 teaspoons vanilla extract

RASPBERRY SAUCE

2 cups fresh raspberries

2 tablespoons sugar

1/2 cup cold water

1. To make the panna cotta: Lightly oil six 1/2-cup (4-ounce) ramekins.

2. Pour the milk into a small bowl and sprinkle the gelatin on top. Let stand to soften the gelatin, about 5 minutes. Meanwhile, bring the cream, sugar, and vanilla to a simmer in a medium saucepan over medium heat. Add the soaked gelatin mixture and reduce the heat to very low. Stir until the gelatin is completely dissolved (do not simmer), about 2 minutes. Divide the cream mixture among the ramekins. Let cool until tepid. Cover each ramekin with plastic wrap and refrigerate until chilled and set, at least 4 hours and up to 2 days.

3. To make the raspberry sauce: Bring the raspberries, sugar, and water to a boil, simmer in a medium nonreactive saucepan, stirring often to dissolve the sugar. Reduce the heat to medium and cook until the juices have thickened slightly, about 3 minutes. Let cool. Rub the sauce through a wire mesh sieve into another bowl. Cover and refrigerate until chilled, at least 2 hours and up to 2 days.

4. To serve, run a dinner knife around the inside of each panna cotta. Hold a dessert plate over the ramekin. Hold and invert the ramekin and plate together and give them a sharp shake to unmold the panna cotta onto the plate. Spoon the raspberry sauce over each and serve chilled.

Chocolate and Hazelnut Gelato

MAKES ABOUT 1 QUART

If you have ever had Italian gelato, you know that it is like American ice cream ... and it is not like American ice cream. The main difference is that the flavors in the Italian version are much stronger, thanks to reduced amounts of fatty cream and sweet sugar and no eggs, all of which tend to mask the other ingredients when you use a heavy hand. Here is a chocolate and hazelnut gelato that has "Italy" written all over it. You will need an ice-cream maker for this, but there are many reasonably priced models on the market.

2½ cups whole milk

½ cup heavy cream

¾ cup cocoa powder, either natural or Dutch-process

¾ cup sugar

3 tablespoons cornstarch

½ cup toasted and coarsely chopped hazelnuts (see Note)

1. Mix the milk and cream together in a liquid measuring cup. Whisk the cocoa powder, sugar, and cornstarch together in a large bowl. Gradually whisk in enough of the milk mixture (about ¾ cup) to dissolve the cornstarch and make a thin paste.

2. Transfer the remaining milk to a medium heavy-bottomed saucepan and bring to a simmer over medium heat. Whisk the hot milk mixture into the cocoa mixture, and return it to the saucepan. Bring to a full boil over medium heat, whisking constantly. Return to the bowl and cover with plastic wrap pressed directly on the surface to discourage a skin forming. Poke a few slits in the plastic wrap with the tip of a knife. Refrigerate until chilled, at least 4 hours or overnight. (Or place the bowl in a larger bowl of iced water to cool completely.)

3. Transfer the cooled cocoa mixture to an ice-cream maker and freeze according to the manufacturer's directions. During the last few minutes, mix in the hazelnuts. Scrape the gelato into a covered container and freeze in the freezer for at least 2 hours or up to 2 days to firm. Scoop into bowl and serve.

NOTE: To toast the hazelnuts, spread them in a single layer on a rimmed baking sheet. Bake in a preheated 350°F oven, stirring occasionally, until the skins are cracked and the flesh underneath is toasted brown, about 12 minutes. Wrap the hot hazelnuts in a clean kitchen towel and let cool for 10 minutes. Using the towel, rub off as much as the skins as possible, but don't worry if some skin is remaining. Let cool completely before chopping.

Strawberries with Cannoli Cream

MAKES 6 TO 8 SERVINGS; ABOUT 2 CUPS CANNOLI CREAM

We sell a lot of cannoli at Patsy's. We have a bakery make the shells for us, and I recommend that you buy yours, too. Everyone loves our house-made filling. Somewhere along the line, we discovered that the ricotta cream is an amazing dip for fresh strawberries. Now, we serve it almost every day at our family lunch table when we all get together for a meal between lunch and dinner service about 3 P.M.

CANNOLI CREAM

1 pound whole-milk ricotta cheese, preferably fresh

²/₃ cup sugar

Zest of ¹/₂ orange

¹/₂ teaspoon vanilla extract

¹/₄ semisweet miniature chocolate chips

1¹/₂ tablespoons finely chopped candied citron

1. To make the cannoli cream: Set a wire mesh sieve over a medium bowl and line it with paper towels. Put the ricotta in the bowl and top with a paper towel and a saucer or bowl that fits inside the sieve. Refrigerate and let the excess whey drain into the bowl. Discard the whey. (Draining the whey is the secret to our cannoli cream. Some cooks use impastata, a thick ricotta cheese made specifically for desserts, but I find it too grainy. This method gives smooth results, even with commercial grocery-store ricotta.)

2. Beat the drained ricotta, sugar, orange zest, and vanilla in a medium bowl with a handheld electric mixer on high speed until the mixture looks a bit fluffier than when you started, about 1½ minutes. Using a rubber spatula, fold in the chocolate chips and citron.

3. Transfer to a bowl and cover. Refrigerate until chilled, at least 2 hours or up to 2 days. Serve chilled.

Grandma Josie's Cream Puffs

MAKES 2 DOZEN; 8 TO 12 SERVINGS

My wife's mother, lovingly called Grandma Josie by our kids, is an excellent cook, and we all enjoy just about everything she whips up. These miniature cream puffs are a treat that she seems to create in the blink of an eye. She saves time by making the filling from instant vanilla pudding. You can substitute your favorite flavor (chocolate pudding with orange zest is nice), or use 2 cups of the Pastry Cream or Cannoli Cream on pages 151 and 190.

FILLING

1 cup heavy cream

1 cup whole milk

One 3.4–ounce package instant vanilla pudding and pie filling

CREAM PUFFS

2 cups water

1/2 cup (1 stick) unsalted butter, cut into 8 tablespoon–size pieces

1 tablespoon granulated sugar

1/4 teaspoon salt

1 cup all–purpose flour

4 large eggs, at room temperature, beaten to blend

Confectioners' sugar, for dusting

1. To make the filling: Whisk the cream, milk, and pudding mix together in a medium bowl until thickened, about 2 minutes. Cover and refrigerate until chilled, at least 2 hours and up to 1 day.

2. To make the cream puffs: Preheat the oven to 400°F. Line a large rimmed baking sheet with parchment paper. Bring the water, butter, granulated sugar, and salt to a boil in a medium saucepan over high heat, stirring occasionally to help the butter melt by the time the water boils. Reduce the heat to medium. Add the flour all at once and stir briskly with a wooden spoon to make a stiff dough. Stir until the dough is beginning to film the bottom of the saucepan, about 1½ minutes. Transfer to a large bowl and let cool for 5 minutes. Using a hand held mixer set on medium speed are whisk, beat in the eggs in four additions, letting the first addition be absorbed into the dough before adding another.

3. Fit a large pastry bag with a ½-inch fluted pastry tip. Transfer the warm dough to the bag. Pipe 2 dozen mounds of dough, spacing them about 1 inch apart, on the parchment paper–lined baking sheet. (Or drop mounds of dough from a tablespoon onto the parchment paper.) Tamp down any pointed tops with a moistened fingertip.

4. Bake for 15 minutes. Reduce the oven temperature to 325°F and continue baking until the puffs are golden brown and crisp, about 20 minutes more. Let cool completely on the baking sheet.

5. Using a serrated knife, cut each puff in half crosswise, keeping track of the tops and bottoms. Transfer the chilled filling to the cleaned pastry bag fitted with the pastry tip. Divide and pipe the fillings among the puff bottoms and replace the tops. (Or spoon the filling into the puff bottoms.) Refrigerate until serving time. Just before serving, dust confectioners' sugar through a wire mesh sieve over the tops of the puffs. Serve chilled.

Patsy's Italian restaurant is a New York institution. Family owned for generations, it feels like home and the food rivals anything momma used to make. I love it, and the Scognamillos, who make the restaurant the great place it is.

—Tony Danza

Rice Pudding Tart
with Dried Cherries

MAKES 8 SERVINGS

When you need a special dessert for a family dinner, I recommend this crostata filled with creamy Arborio rice pudding and dried cherries. You won't believe how easy it is to pull this off—the dough doesn't have to rolled out and is simply pressed into the tart pan.

FILLING

1/3 cup dried tart cherries

2 tablespoons maraschino liqueur (see Note), kirsch, or golden rum

2 1/2 cups whole milk

1/4 cup Arborio rice

1/4 cup granulated sugar

2 tablespoons unsalted butter

2 large eggs plus 1 large egg yolk

1/4 teaspoon vanilla extract

TART DOUGH

1 cup all-purpose flour, preferably unbleached

2 tablespoons granulated sugar

1/8 teaspoon salt

1. To make the filling: Combine the dried cherries and maraschino liqueur in a small bowl. Let the cherries soak and soften while preparing the crostada.

2. Bring the milk, rice, granulated sugar, and butter to a simmer in a medium heavy-bottomed saucepan over medium heat. Reduce the heat to medium-low and partially cover the saucepan. Simmer, stirring often, until the rice is very tender, about 25 minutes. Remove from the heat and let cool.

3. Meanwhile, make the tart dough: Position a rack in the bottom third of the oven, and preheat the oven to 400°F.

4. Mix the flour, granulated sugar, and salt in a medium bowl. Add the butter and cut it in with a pastry blender or two knives until the mixture resembles coarse crumbs with some pea-size pieces of butter. Stir in the yolk mixture and mix until the dough clumps together. Press the dough firmly and evenly into a 9-inch tart pan with a removable bottom. Freeze for 15 to 20 minutes.

5. Line the dough with a sheet of aluminum foil and fill the foil with pastry weights or dried beans. Place the tart pan on a large rimmed baking sheet. Bake until the edge of the crust is beginning to brown. Remove from the oven and lift off the foil with the weights. Pierce the crust a few times with a fork and return to the oven, without the foil and weights. Continue baking until the bottom of the dough is just beginning to brown, about 10 minutes more. Remove from the oven again.

6 tablespoons (¾ stick) cold unsalted butter, cut into small cubes

1 large egg yolk beaten with 1 tablespoon cold water

Confectioners' sugar, for dusting

6. Stir the soaked cherries with their liqueur, whole eggs, egg yolk, and vanilla into the cooled rice mixture. Pour into the crust. Return to the oven and continue baking until the filling is set when the pan is shaken lightly, 35 to 40 minutes. Transfer to a wire cooling rack and let cool. (The cooled tart can be covered and refrigerated for 1 day. Let stand at room temperature for 1 hour before serving.)

7. Remove the sides of the pan. Sift confectioners' sugar through a fine-mesh wire sieve over the tart. Cut into wedges and serve.

NOTE: Maraschino is a clear liqueur made from Dalmatian cherries (Dalmatia used to be part of the Venetian Empire). It bears no resemblance to American maraschino cherries.

Whenever I want an authentic home-cooked Italian meal I go to Patsy's Italian Restaurant.
—Sean "Diddy" Combs

Peach Crostata

MAKES 6 TO 8 SERVINGS

A crostata can be made in a tart pan for a finished, "bakery" appearance, or it can be shaped free-form for a rustic look. This is a summertime crostata, for when local peaches are in season and you want to eat them for every meal before they are gone.

DOUGH

1 cup all-purpose flour, preferably unbleached, plus more for rolling out

2 tablespoons sugar

1/4 teaspoon salt

8 tablespoons (1 stick) cold unsalted butter, cut into small cubes

3 tablespoons ice-cold water, as needed

FILLING

4 ripe peaches, peeled (see Note), pitted, and cut into 1/2-inch wedges

2 tablespoons cornstarch

2 tablespoons sugar

1 tablespoon unsalted butter, cut into small cubes

1. To make the dough: Mix the flour, sugar, and salt in a medium bowl. Add the butter and cut it in with a pastry blender or two knives until the mixture resembles coarse crumbs with some pea-size pieces of butter. Stir in enough water to moisten the flour mixture until it clumps together. Press the dough together: It should be moist and pliable enough to roll out without cracking, so add a little more water, if needed. Gather the dough into a thick disk, wrap in plastic wrap, and refrigerate until chilled, at least 1 hour and up to 1 day. (The dough is easiest to roll out after 1 or 2 hours of chilling. If it is very chilled and hard, let stand at room temperature for 15 minutes before rolling.)

2. To make the filling. Toss the peaches, cornstarch, and sugar together in a medium bowl.

3. Preheat the oven to 375°F. Line a large rimmed baking sheet with parchment paper.

4. On a lightly floured work surface, roll out the dough into a 13-inch-diameter circle. Transfer it to the lined baking sheet. Leaving a 3-inch-wide border, arrange the peach slices in two concentric circles, overlapping as needed, on the dough circle. Fold the exposed crust over the peaches, leaving some peaches exposed in the center. Dot with the butter and pour and juices from the filling bowl over the peach mixture.

5. Bake until the filling juices are bubbling and the crust is golden brown, about 45 minutes. Let cool on the baking sheet for at least 30 minutes. Carefully slide the crostata onto a serving dish. Serve warm or cooled.

NOTE: To peel the peaches, bring a medium saucepan of water to a boil over high heat. Working in batches, add the peaches and boil just until the skin loosens, 30 seconds to 1 minute. Using a slotted spoon, transfer the peaches to a bowl of iced water and let stand until cool enough to handle. Using a small knife, remove the skins.

For "boil-less" peeling, use a swivel-type vegetable peeler to remove the skins from the raw peaches. Use light pressure and work around the circumference of the peach as if you were peeling an apple, moving the peeler in a slight zigzag motion.

If the peach skins are thin and fuzz-free, then you can also opt out of peeling entirely.

"Sal is one of New York's most familiar restaurant chefs and his food is beloved by many. I have had the good fortune to have Sal on my show where he cooked his tasty clams oreganata and baccalà salad, demonstrating why Patsy's is one of New York's favorite eateries. I look forward to trying all of the recipes in this new book."

—*Martha Stewart, founder, Martha Stewart Living Omnimedia*

Apple Fritters

Italians love fried desserts. Apple fritters are a casual dessert, best served to close friends or family in batches, just as they come out of the oil. There isn't any sugar in the batter, so sweet apples work better than tart ones.

1 cup all-purpose flour

1½ teaspoons baking powder

¼ teaspoon salt

1 large egg

¾ cup whole milk, as needed

3 sweet apples, such as Jazz or Gala, peeled, cored, and cut into ⅓-inch rings

Vegetable oil, for deep-frying

Confectioners' sugar, for dusting

1. Pour enough oil into a large saucepan to come halfway up the sides and heat over high heat until it reads 360°F on a deep-frying thermometer. Line a large rimmed baking sheet with a double layer of paper towels.

2. Sift the flour, baking powder, and salt together into a medium bowl. Whisk the egg in a small bowl, add the milk, and whisk again. Pour into the dry ingredients and whisk just until combined. The consistency should be similar to pancake batter; add more milk, if needed.

3. Working in batches, dip the apple rings in the batter to coat. Let the excess batter drip off into the bowl, and transfer the apple rings to the hot oil. Deep-fry, turning halfway through the cooking, until golden brown, about 2½ minutes. Using a wire skimmer or a slotted spoon, transfer the fritters to the paper towel–lined baking sheet. Sift confectioners' sugar through a wire sieve over the fritters and serve immediately.

Afterword

by Peter Scognamillo (Sal's son, age 16)

Peter, age 7, making tiramisu

Cannoli, marinara sauce, zeppoles, meatballs, and any other Italian delicacies that you can think of have surrounded me my whole life. I would like it to stay that way.

Ever since I can remember, I have aspired to follow in my father's footsteps by becoming the head chef at my family's restaurant. Whenever I walk into Patsy's there is a thrilling rush that fills my whole body with joy. I am truly honored to be a part of this family. At least twice a week in the summer, and as much as I can during the school year, I visit my second home, Patsy's Italian Restaurant. During those days, I look at what my great-grandfather had started, what my grandfather carried on, passing the tradition down to my father. I constantly remind myself of how blessed I am to be learning about what Grandpa Patsy did.

Whenever my father is showing me the ropes, he has always reminded me of the three F's—the three reasons why Patsy's remains in business. The first two F's are the food, of course, and Frank Sinatra. Our food is the best I have ever tasted (and, being a chef's son, I have tasted a lot of food). Frank Sinatra was a dear family friend, who we considered a family member, and who promoted Patsy's and will never be forgotten. The third F, and perhaps the most important one, is family. Our restaurant is really just serving food to other family members at the dining room table. We love each other, and treat our customers the same way. Families are forever.

Acknowledgments

I love being a chef. In fact, I love it so much that I always say that I've never worked a day in my life. I also loved writing this, my second cookbook. This book contains several recipes from my extended family. I loved learning the stories behind a recipe from my wife's Sicilian family, or reminiscing about a fond memory associated with one of Grandpa Patsy's traditional dishes. In short, I had fun writing this cookbook.

I wouldn't be where I am today if it wasn't for the courage, hard work, and perseverance of my paternal grandparents, Pasquale (fondly known as "Patsy") and Concetta Scognamillo. They came to this country from Naples, Italy with little more than the recipes from their ancestors. The lessons they instilled about the importance of family, honesty, and loyalty are the foundation of our family today. Thank you, Grandma and Grandpa, for everything.

My father Joe has always been, and will always be, the backbone of Patsy's Italian Restaurant and our family. He has dedicated his entire life to making the restaurant the success that it is, and he continues to work to this day. I aspire to be more like him every day, learning from his wisdom, experience, and strength. Thanks, Dad, for always believing in me.

A very special thanks to my mom, Rose, who has been working alongside my dad for the past twenty-five plus years. Thank you for your love and support throughout the years.

I am eternally grateful to my wife, Lisa, and my two sons, Joseph and Peter, for their unconditional love, unwavering support and endless patience. My wife's faith motivates me to be a better man, and my children's love gives me strength. They are my rock.

I want to give special recognition to my wife's parents, Jo and Pete Bonelli, who have always been there for me. They are my "other parents." I also want to thank my sister, Tina, and her husband, Joe for their encouragement over the years.

Thank you to my cousin Frank and his family, who helped make this cookbook a unique family project.

I am grateful to Rick Rodgers for his creative genius and attention to detail, which make this book a cut above the rest.

Special thanks to Michele Pascetta and Russ Cahill, who help keep the office details of the restaurant running smoothly.

I am very appreciative of my editor Elizabeth Beier, and her assistants Michelle Richter and Anya Lichtenstein for their perseverance and determination in seeing this project through. Thanks for getting me through the rough spots. The same goes for my wonderful agent, Marly Rusoff. Thank you for your support and great advice throughout this process. And a special note of gratitude to the book's copy editor, Leah Stewart.

The beautiful photography was the work of

Jeffrey Gurwin. Thank you for your patience and for being such a perfectionist.

I must say a very special thank you to my life-long dear friend Ben Stiller for writing such a moving foreword to this book. You and your family have always been a very special part of our family.

We love you.

Most of all, thank you to you, my readers, and all those who have supported me throughout the years. With love from my kitchen to yours,

—*Sal*

Photo of Patsy and Concetta, taken by Frank Sinatra from the stage of the Fontainebleau Hotel in Miami.

Everyone Loves
Patsy's Italian Family Cookbook

"Who could be better than Sal Scognamillo to keep Italian–American food culture alive? His customers know it and that's why they keep coming back to Patsy's. Now you can create these beloved dishes in your own kitchen with Sal as your guide. Everyone who loves Italian–American food should have this book in their kitchen library."

—Mary Ann Esposito

"My parents, Judy Garland and Vincente Minnelli, first brought me to Patsy's when I was twelve years old. That was the beginning of a lifetime friendship and a wonderful lifelong dining experience."

—Liza Minnelli

"I can assure you that if you are able to cook these dishes only half as well at home as Sal cooks them at Patsy's, you'll never go out to another restaurant again (except for Patsy's)."

—Philip Roth

"There is no place in New York City—much less the world—like Patsy's. Every time I walk into that restaurant, I feel like I'm home. My husband, Jimmy, and I love Patsy's so much that we had our rehearsal dinner there the night before our wedding. Between the food, the generosity, the friendship, and the warmth of Patsy's, it was one of the best nights of our lives!"

—Lisa Lampanelli

"A cookbook triumph from the chef at Patsy's! You can't beat the food, and the recipes in this book."

—Mary Higgins Clark

"My first memories of going to Patsy's are with my mother, Lucille Ball, and my stepfather, Gary Morton. Mom just adored the place, the family ownership, and the private room upstairs where she could just enjoy a meal without always being interrupted for an autograph. Mom would never turn down a fan, even if she had a mouthful of spaghetti!"

—Lucie Arnaz

"Patsy's always has an exciting atmosphere and I have wonderful memories of their really authentic Italian food."

—Mel Brooks

Index